Lovebound

By

Regina Moody

Lovebound

By Regina Moody

Published by Destiny House Publishing, LLC

Copyright ©2013 Regina Moody

ISBN 9781936867486

Unless otherwise stated, all scripture quotations are from the Holy Bible, King James Version. Scripture references that do not have the Bible version noted are the author's paraphrase.

Cover design and Publication Layout: Destiny House Publishing, LLC

Artwork from Dreamstime

Editing: Destiny House Publishing, LLC

ALL RIGHTS RESERVED

All rights reserved under International Copyright law. No part of this book may be reproduced or transmitted in any form or by any means: electronic, mechanical, including photocopying and recording, or by any information storage and retrieval system, without permission in writing from the publisher.

Printed in the United States of America

For information:

Destiny House Publishing, LLC

www.destinyhousepublishing.com

email: inquiry@destinyhousepublishing.com

P.O. Box 19774 Detroit, MI 48219 888-890-9455

DEDICATION

Love Bound

This book is dedicated to my husband Mickey, the love of my life. Thank you for sharing your life and love with me; and to our son Lee, you have taught me a lot as I fumbled through motherhood. Thank you for your love and for the laughter you brought into my life. I love you both more than mere penned words could ever express - always have, always will...

There are so many reasons why I chose to call my story "love bound". It is love that binds us all together and it is love itself; God's love that holds us together. Mickey once told me "your own act is a hard one to follow." For so much of my life I was expected to act a certain way or to think a certain way but this is my story as I have chosen to tell it. There have been moments in my life that stand out. Those moments are as clear as Waterford crystal in my mind's eye and there are moments that have grown dim. I suppose that most of our lives are like that. Everyone's life is lived in moments rather than in years. It's often mere moments that we recall most vividly. My first memories began around the age of one. They are good memories for the most part. Even as I write this, memories of my granddaddy leap into my mind. He loved me and enjoyed spending time with me. At the early age of one my granddaddy was the first impression of what love looked like to me. We all come into the world seeking and searching for love and in his gentle eyes I found it. I stayed by his side as much as I could. He showered me with love and attention. I was "spoiled" to say the least. I recall the times that he took me into the yard to feed the chickens. He had an old homemade boat anchor, which looked like a big rock with a chain in the end of it. He'd pull it about with the chain and use it as a table to crack oyster shells on. Then he'd let me help him feed the shells to the chickens and I'd feed them as quickly as my small hands would allow me to. He told me that those shells are what made the eggs stronger. I believed him because in my eyes my granddaddy knew everything! We would go out and check on ole "Queen", a mule that he'd had for years. Queen was much too old to plow by this time but still he kept her and treated her good until the day she died. I remember the way that he'd "remind" my grandma to "remember to get my girls cream" as he so lovingly called my ice cream. He was everything to me. He petted and protected me. Nothing could hurt or harm me as long as he was around. I was often scolded for taking my food to his little fold up table. My grandma kept a fold up table near his chair for his meals and that was where I chose to take my meals as well. He would clear his throat and tell her over her rebuke to "leave her alone she is okay, she is not bothering me". As much as I loved my granddaddy I could not imagine that there was someone who loved him more. My grandma or "ma" as I called her loved him with everything in her. She was his love and his protector. What I didn't understand was that he was real sick. He had a diagnosis of emphysema. I had grown into a toddler of three and as I'd grown, his illness had too. Quietly I watched as two of my uncles helped him walk to a car. One stood on each side giving him support enough to stand. Their gaits were slow but somehow they managed to get him into the awaiting car. Later I learned that they had taken him to the hospital. The smell of the hospital lobby was seared into my little mind. I didn't know what a hospital was really or how long that he'd be there. After what seemed like forever to me they finally took me "to see my granddaddy" but it was not what I had imagined. I was too young to be permitted into his room. He had asked to see me and the hospital staff had reluctantly agreed to let us visit at the window. I never got to hug him or get behind his back to keep others from "getting me" again. I was taken outside of his window. I watched him place his hand on the inside of the window and from the outside of it I put my hand against his and that is the way they forced us to say "goodbye" He never got to come back home and I felt lost and alone. I did not understand that God was with me because in my thoughts it was God that took my granddaddy from me. Everyone kept telling me that he was with God in Heaven. I did not understand why God would take him from me. I wasn't brought up in church. We did attend sporadically in years to come but almost never the same church for long. Talk about lost. My grandma was lost. After my granddaddy died she fell apart for a while. She did not know what to do with herself, let alone me. She used to keep us but for a while she was no longer emotionally equipped to do that. By this time I had a brother, Louie. At three years old I became "the big sister". I learned that we had other grandparents. They were called Great grandparents. Their house was like an adventure for me. Both of them were nice to us so I liked it when we got to go to their house. They sometimes kept us while momma and daddy worked. We'd have to get up pretty early though but we'd get to go back to bed once we arrived. She was a real short lady with the blackest hair I'd ever saw on a grandma. I was told it was because of the Indian in her bloodline. He was a tall slim man. Both of them were soft spoken and he rarely spoke at all. I do recall trying not to go to the bathroom when we first got there so that after a little while I could announce that I had to go! You see I had learned that they had this peculiar thing that they called a "slop jar", and if I had to go to the bathroom after I was tucked in I got the privilege of using it! Now up until this point "slop" was a word that I had known that my first granddaddy called food that he had given to his hogs. He even had a wagon that he'd hook Queen up to when he went around town to collect folk's slop. As a child I thought that picking up slop was okay, it wasn't until later that I learned that it had shame associated with it. My great grandma humored me. She never seemed annoyed at my amusement of the way things were at their home. Their real bathroom was actually built onto their back porch. The slop jar was supposed to serve the purpose of keeping you from having to go out into the cold to relieve yourself. If memory serves me well they did have the remains of an old outhouse still there in their backyard. My great granddad was a kind man. He would take me with him to feed the cows while my little brother stayed inside. He was too little to help but he'd say I was "big enough to help" My help consisted of him sitting me on the fence to watch him feed the cows then following him over to the old store near the cows. He'd purchase me a drink (Coke) from the machine outside of the store. The machines were strange to me. He'd put in the change and I'd have to try and pull out the Coke. I pulled with all of my might but in the end he'd always have to grab a hold to the Coke bottles neck and get it out for me. The Cokes were colder than they are now and I recall thanking God that he was strong enough to get the drink out. Other than thanking God for my little brother, at this point I don't remember really thanking God for anything. We didn't get to stay long with these grandparents either I don't recall why. I know we had several "real babysitters" before we started staying with "ma" again. Things began to happen to me during my childhood that I will not elaborate on except to say that I was no longer protected from the evil of others. In their defense my parents had no idea of the things that I had endured. Fear kept me quiet. My parents seemed happy for a while. They seemed almost like children themselves at times. I will never forget the good memories of how they played together when things were good. Once they wet each other with the water hose and chased one another into the backyard I saw daddy scoop her up into her arms just as the neighbor lady peered through her window. He told me years later his memory of this and how he almost dropped my momma when he heard me yell to the neighbor," If you want to see them better just go to the back door!" because he was laughing so hard. The fishing trips at Long Bridge stand out to me because that is something that daddy taught us to love. Christmas was great too we always got a lot of gifts, even toys back then. The last Christmas in my childhood with my mom is still a vivid memory for me. I got an organ and we pecked out the notes to "silent night" and sang it together. I have a lot of beach memories as my mom loved the beach and we went often. Louie and I (my brother) had a lot of fun we'd build sandcastles, look for shells, cover each other with sand and 'Ride the waves" in the ocean. By this time I was nine and he six. The real waves were just about to begin in our lives. I was shy and timid probably somewhat because of the abuse I had received at the hands of others. I hung my head when spoken to; never did I feel at ease looking people directly in the eyes. Fear was not my friend and yet it was my constant companion. I tried "to be good" and do well for my parents. I tried hard just to fit in with others only this was not an easy task for me. At the encouragement of my mother I became a majorette. She tried to pull me from the shell that was so rapidly growing around me. I went out for cheerleader and much to my surprise I was chosen to be on the squad. I don't think my mom knew I was chosen because by the time the season started she was gone. People tend to do the best that they can. I realize that now as an adult that they did their best to hold things together. In all marriages troubles come and if we aren't grounded in the word those troubles may become insurmountable. The day that my mom left was hard for us all. The fight between the two of them was terrible to see and the yelling was not easy to hear but the silence that followed was probably the most difficult. Ma tried to tell them to stop fighting and work it out. I felt that the silence was because of me because I was crying so hard I shook and Ma told them "ya'll are going to make her have a nervous breakdown if you don't stop". The fighting calmed down and we drove momma home "to get her things". We sat in the car for a little while in front of our home not sure of anything. A young man stopped beside our car to "make sure we were okay". I had no idea at the time who he was but later I learned that he was the man that I now refer to as my husband. Mickey Moody walked into my life at the first time when I was nine years old. Webster defines divorce as the legal dissolution of a marriage; the complete separation of things. Pretty cut and dry or so it sounds. The thing is that it never is so cut and dry. We are all complex creations. That is how God designed us. Nothing about human relationships is simple. Learning how to relate to one another sometimes takes us a lifetime. The next few years were difficult to say the least. At the young age of nine I began trying to hold everything together. Everyone and everything around me was falling apart. My daddy cried himself to sleep a lot of nights. In the beginning he read the bible to me but because he was in such pain and couldn't make it stop the bible reading was given up shortly. He sought for other ways to comfort himself. He was struggling just to survive the pain he was feeling and he did have two mouths to feed. It must have felt like the weight of the world was on his shoulders. I really believe that he thought they'd work things out and get back together but that was never to be. He had given my mom our car, which meant that he had to walk or ride a bike to the store. I suppose he had gotten a ride to work but to be honest I don't recall every detail. I do remember us going to talk to some of mom's friends. I suppose he was searching for answers of his own. As for myself I have found that the answers that I sought rested within me all of the time. We all have had times in our lives when we've felt alone and abandoned. We all have had times that we were hurt. I believe that in facing our demons we strip them of their power over us. It is my hope that as you read this you will be able to see God's hand in my life and in yours. Our Lord restores us but it is not always an easy process. If you are willing to be healed of your hurts God is ready to help you. You must first learn to trust Him at his word. Learning to trust anyone, even God was hard for me. I tried to buy groceries for the first time at the age of nine. I say tried to because can you just for a moment try to imagine what type of groceries a child of nine buys? Needless to say I got into trouble for my unwise purchases. I had to learn how to do things that were beyond my years. My dad or a relative would drive me about to the places to pay bills and I'd go inside and pay the bills. Who needed to play house? I was living it! I still had moments when I got to enjoy my childhood. I had cousins that came down for the weekend and they would stay at Ma's with us. Louie and I had to stay at Ma's most of the time though because Ma insisted that our old house was haunted so she refused to stay there anymore. Daddy kept the house. It came in handy for his company or parties. Not every day was a party for him. He worked hard jobs to keep us fed but he did enjoy his time on weekends to de-stress. After the divorce daddy found comfort in drinking and getting together with others that had been through similar things. I am proud to say that he no longer drinks. I do understand now as an adult that divorce is like a death and it hurts even the toughest of people. I have bittersweet memories of Ma's place but I do have good ones too. Like I said earlier we four cousins got together almost every other weekend. Like kids do we fought from time to time then we'd cry when they had to leave. Imagine that! There for a while the fights got so bad that the adults broke down and got us boxing gloves and made us really fight. For some reason they thought this to be a solution! Ma's place seemed to have everything fun! She had a big pear tree in her front yard that we were "forbidden" to climb. Often the images of four children could be seen jumping from that tree when Ma opened the screen door to check on us. There was another place that was "off limits" to the four of us, it was called the trussel. We had to walk down the railroad tracks to get to this place. We did not mind having to walk train tracks. We actually liked walking on the rails themselves. My brother walked them so much that he had actually developed the skill of running in on the rails. I was not as sure footed as he but we turned it into game by seeing who could walk the farthest or run the fastest on them. We all gained the skill of getting back from the trussel to Ma's yard as fast as possible. Then of course the real skill was trying to appear innocent, as if we were right there nearby all the time. The trussel was a bridge with little steps built on the sides. It rested over water. It served not only as a bridge, but also as a safe place to get off the tracks if the train was on its way. We all knew to respect the train. I had been taught by my granddad to respect it and to bend my little arm and mimic the driver pulling the cord of the horn. Often, I could get the train driver to blow the whistle for me. All of us knew the danger that the train could be if we didn't get off of the tracks in time. We liked to skip rocks into the waters that drifted beneath the bridge. Within those dark waters lived all sorts of animals. To our amazement once we discovered a large alligator turtle creeping back into those waters. We all thought it would be an adventure to catch him. He was huge but all four of us caught hold of him as best as we could and we pulled with all of our might. Needless to say he was strong! All of our effort was wasted on him the four of us finally gave up when we couldn't get the big ole thing from the security of his home waters. Now what in the world we thought we were going to do with the thing was beyond me! I thank God to this day that we were not bitten. When we all got together we were rowdy kids. We sought fun and discovered all kind of adventures sprang from the unity of our minds. We were always getting into something. There was a great place for us to play behind Ma's property. It wasn't her land but we couldn't resist sneaking onto it. This place we all called the "tractor graveyard". At the graveyard, there were old tractors and old cars that no longer worked. We'd play for hours there in those old things. I was more interested in the cars than the tractors and in my mind I drove to all of the places that were places that I could only dream of going. Woods surrounded our house. There was only one dirt road in to our place unless you came through the trails through the woods. We loved exploring the woods. We built us a special place in the woods and we called it "the little pond". In reality it was no pond at all just a big hole that we all dug out and when the rains came it filled it with water. We put old tires in it and floated across it by propelling the tires with long sticks/poles. My brother loved the woods. Louie got to know those woods around our place so well that he excelled in hunting. He could walk up on others in the woods before they knew he was anywhere around. They'd comment on his Indian like steps. Sometimes Louie would convince me to go hunting with him. We never seemed to have the luck that he had when he went alone and yet still he'd want me to go. We'd just sit together in the tree stand and talk when it became obvious that we were not going to kill a deer. I valued those times with my brother. We spent a lot of time together. We didn't have all of the things that other kids had but we had each other. We enjoyed watching movies together. Daddy would let us rent a VCR on weekends sometimes when we had the extra money. We'd sit up all night long watching one movie after another. During my childhood our TV was not like the ones we have now. We had about three stations available on it, if the weather was good. We would have to go outside and "turn the antenna" to get a clear picture sometimes even when the weather was good. Turning the antenna consisted of someone going outside and another person staying inside to monitor the picture on the TV and the person inside had to adjust the Rabbit ears on the TV. This was the small antenna on the TV, which we usually wrapped with tinfoil to aide in getting us a clear picture. Man times really have changed! We were limited as far as things to do for entertainment. Louie started typing stories and sharing them with me. He really had a talent for it but he would usually tear up the stories after he read them to me. I loved a good story. I read a lot of books. When I read I found that I could escape the person that I was and I welcomed the escape. I never felt at ease with people and there was security within my books. We had some rough days like everyone does. I think that for the most part the troubles that we learn to overcome shapes us into what God intends us to become. Both Louie and I blamed ourselves for things that were not our fault. Ma loved an occasional beer. I would caution her about the dangers of mixing her heart medicine with alcohol. She'd respond to me by telling me "she knew better than that and that she had left off her heart medicine for the day" Sometimes she'd overdo the beer. She would sing "I'll fly away" and dance about. The more that she drank; the more that I'd find myself wishing that she would fly away. She'd say harsh things to us when she drank too much like how she was "at her home and if we didn't like it we could go to ours" I hated that because I felt like I no longer had a home of my own. We just didn't seem to "belong" anywhere anymore. A lot of time I felt like I was in the way. The drinking reproduced the grief of my granddaddy's death in her mind. She'd end up holding granddads picture and crying herself to sleep. After the effects of the alcohol wore off she'd tell us that she was sorry. She'd try to reassure us that she wanted us there with her. She was not a spring chicken and I know it must have been an awful strain on her raising two small children at her age. She had some old fashioned ways of thinking and she grounded those thoughts into me at an early age. Some of those thoughts I have overcome and still some of them creep in even after all of these years. I was never permitted to wear the color red, as it "was a harlot's color". We were not allowed to talk on the phone later than eight pm. Boys called girls back then not the other way around. If a girl called a boy you could just about imagine her wearing red. We not only were behind technology when it came to our TV but our phone was on what was called "a party line". This was a line that several people from different households had to share. We could pick up the phone and hear someone from another house talking on our line. We were a long distance from the Internet but this was our information highway. Sometimes it was pure accident to hear others talking and sometimes Ma was honing her eavesdropping skills. This was an art that we were familiar with. Ma found pleasure in listening to the others on our line although she would never admit to it. Her phone was her lifeline because she seldom left her house. She did leave once a month for her regular doctor's checkup. She'd get herself all dressed up. She'd even wear her top teeth. She'd only wear the top ones on her outings because the bottom plate hurt her mouth. Not having her teeth did not limit her eating in any way. She could even chew gum. She would do all of her running about on the same day as her doctor's appointment. Her running about consisted of going to the doctor, the grocery store, the drug store, and to Miranda's department store. Occasionally she would set up a hair appointment. She was a practical woman and never did many things that she deemed frivolous. She had survived hard times and seemed to keep herself braced for more if they were to be on the horizon. She married young once before my granddaddy. She told me about him a couple of times when I was older. He was a mean man and she was afraid of him. She was so afraid that after he ran her through the woods one night she returned home to her mother and dad's home. By this time she was pregnant she was ashamed to go home expecting a baby but she feared for her life so she never returned to him. Back then divorce was not thought of and she felt trapped to the man. He later was in an accident and drowned so she was then "free" to marry my granddaddy. She loved him with all of her heart. There was nothing that she wouldn't do for "Red" as she called him, including fight. She was crazy jealous over him from all that I've been told. I guess this was the first image that I had of true love. I do remember her washing his feet. She was by no means "liberated". She honored him in life and even after his death. She told me that a woman was never to show her love openly for a man. It was unladylike plus it revealed your weakness for them. She was a woman of strength and did not want to appear weak in any sense of the word. I don't remember her ever telling my granddaddy that she loved him in front of anyone. She said some things were to be done in private. They had seven children and lost a set of twins. She showed her love by doing things for you not by telling you how she felt. I don't remember being hugged too much as a child. She did take extra care of us when we were sick though. She'd cover us with those heavy handmade quilts and make us stay on the couch "where she could watch us" She made the best chicken soup from scratch not from a can. Although she could be as rough as a cob she did have a gentle mothering side that came out at times. She was protective over my brother and me, and she never set out to hurt us in any way. I realize its only hurting people that hurt others. She kept hogs as long as she was able. She loved those dirty things! We'd raise them up from pigs and once in a while they'd take one to be butchered. She'd cook almost anything. I laugh even now at the thought of the chipmunk that she cooked to teach my brother that if you kill it you eat it! He had mistaken it for a squirrel. I don't know a lot of facts about chipmunks but they must be good for your eyesight. After she made my brother eat the one he shot, he never again mistakenly shot one for a squirrel. In her odd way she taught us that every life has value. I can't help but wonder if she ever realized the value of her own life. I know that I did not learn the value my own life until years later. We can't blame others if our lives are not what we want them to be. It is God that enables us to fulfill our destiny but we must learn to look to him for help in doing so. Sometimes it is not others that hold us back from our destiny but it is often times ourselves. When my brother Louie was just getting interested in girls, one caught his eye. He confided in me one morning that as we walked to school that he was going to ask her to "go together". He was too young to date but all of the kids back then that liked each other would say that they were "going together". This did not mean that they physically went anywhere together. They'd walk together around the schoolyard as a couple and that was about the extent of it. That morning we laughed and talked about him and this girl all the way to school. He was so excited and happy. As we arrived at school, I wished him luck and we went our separate ways. In just a brief amount of time Louie came running towards me and he was crying. Oh no, I thought she has just broken my little brother's heart. It turned out so much worse than I could have imagined. She had been in an accident. She had been shot and killed. Louie never got to tell her how he felt about her. Grief enveloped him. The girl's funeral was awful. We had arrived about the same time the hearse did and Louie was asked to help carry her casket into the church. The man that had asked him to help had no idea how hard it was for him to do this. I could just about see his knees buckle as he reached for the cold steel casket. Louie grieved for a long time. I found letters that he had written her after her death. He wanted to be with her and that made me afraid. I'd tried to watch after him and protect him all of his life and yet I couldn't stop this pain. I was really worried about my brother. You see in our house amidst all of the drama was laughter but for a long time Louie's laughter ceased. The laughter in our lives was important. It seemed to dull the things that we were feeling. In our family everyone learned the skill of pranks and telling jokes. My son seems to have been blessed with the skill of making people laugh. We all have coping mechanisms in us placed there by God himself. The word says that he knew us before we were placed inside our mother's womb. He created us with everything that we need not only to survive but also to fulfill our purpose in this life. Finding our purpose may take some of us years to do. Things that we do not understand happen to us but God's grace is sufficient. He can help us through anything that comes our way. There is nothing too big or hard for God. I recall once being upset as a child because I wanted to "pet the new biddies but the mother hen wouldn't let me". As luck would have it my Uncle Melton saw my distress and came to my aide. He always had advice for me. He told me if I'd wet the hen she'd get up and I could pet the new biddies all that I wanted to. In my ignorance I proceeded to do just that. I was small but I was determined. I struggled for some time with the water hose but finally I had drug it all of the to the mother hen's nest. When I got close enough I turned it on and placed my little thumb over the end of the hose so that I could spray the hen down good. I soaked her good but when she got up I no longer cared to pet the biddies. She headed straight for my skinny little legs! I can honestly say that I do know what the term "madder than a wet setting hen" means first hand! I ran to Ma crying about what the hen did to me. When she asked me where I had come up with such a plan Uncle Melton wasn't as pleased with his joke as he first was. He told Ma "I didn't think she'd really do it" but still he laughed. Ma herself was a jokester. I have heard stories about some of the pranks she pulled. Once when my granddaddy had caught her repairing an electric fence, he turned it on as she was attempting to retie it. She didn't get mad instead she got even. About one year later the tables turned. Granddaddy was working on the fence. He had forgotten his little prank but Ma hadn't forgotten. She had bided her time and then when the opportunity presented itself she flipped the "on" switch just as he was retying the fence. Proof that what goes around comes around. What you sow you will ultimately reap! My daddy still laughs when he recalls this story about his parents. Daddy's favorite joke was "pull my finger" and it turned out to be a stinking joke. Long before caller id was thought of Louie and our cousin Durrell came up with what they thought was a perfect prank. They would go through the phone book and pick a random number. One of them would call the number and ask for a factious person. Of course they were told that they had the wrong number. This would be repeated several times by calling the same number over and over again. Each time they would be told a little more firmly that" there was no person with that name at that residence". When the person on the receiving end of the prank was good and mad the other one would call one last time and tell them that they were the factious name and go on to ask "have I had any messages or calls?" After what I am sure was an irate response they'd hang up and laugh together. We tried to find ways to "get" one another too. After one of our many fishing trips Durrell thought it would be amusing to put fish heads into his sister, Charlotte's shoes. So that the bloody fish head couldn't be seen he took care to push it way up into the toe of her tennis shoes. Like I said earlier they often spent the weekend with us. Being from the country, we all loved to go "barefooted". On Monday morning Charlotte tried getting her feet into her tennis shoes. It was a school morning and we were all getting ready. She of course met resistance trying to get into those shoes so she reached her hand into the toe of them and out came a smelly fish head! No one had to tell her who had done it either. Immediately she started yelling for her brother. Their daddy overheard the ruckus. Durrell tried to explain "he'd thought she'd found them by now!" How Uncle Melton kept a straight face, I will never know. Charlotte had no choice but wear those shoes to school so she borrowed some perfume from me. It didn't make much difference though no perfume could mask the smell of three-day-old fish heads. There were things that did not start out as jokes but ended up getting laughs over the years to come. For example the time I was "teaching Charlotte to drive" and she took off a whole side of bark from one of ma's pecan trees. Either she was not a good student or I wasn't a good teacher. My dad's car was damaged and he fussed about it but in the end he actually helped us nail the bark back onto the tree to "keep her from getting into trouble". That slab of bark did eventually fall from the tree and it left the tree scarred. I joke that it's Charlotte's memorial. Back then we all drove before we were licensed to. We'd practice anywhere the adults let us, which usually was fields or dirt roads. We rode around without seat belts, as they were not "the law" back then. To have put on a seat belt we'd have had to dig them from underneath the seats anyways. That is where they were put so they'd "be out of the way". It was a common sight to see underage drivers on the roads in my home town (Samson, Alabama). Often "the law" would just throw up a hand and wave at us as we drove past them. Having the ability to drive around town did make it easier for me to go and pay bills or get groceries for the family. A neighbor girl took us cousins all for a spin. She had just gotten her license. We raced down a dirt road near ma's property and the girl managed to drive us right into a ditch. A police officer happened by. As we climbed into the back seat of the police car Durrell started protesting "but I can't go to jail, I have a turtle to take care of!" The officer laughed out loud and took us home. I don't recall how the girl got her car out of the ditch I was just glad to be out of her car and back at home. Durrell did indeed have a turtle. We all had strange animals over the years as "pets". We had a make shift "pen" of old tin we "built" ourselves where we'd house animals from the wild that we captured. Often we had turtles/gophers housed inside this pen. We liked animals so we'd cage them up so we could "take care of them". Aunt Alma (my grandma's sister/our great aunt) would discover our "pets" and she'd slip around and turn them all loose. She'd lecture us on the "sins of penning up wild animals". Her lectures were not always so easy to follow. Her speech was impaired. Aunt Alma was difficult to understand in a lot of ways. We'd recapture the animals. We liked to just play with them and feed them too. We feed blackberries to gophers and some of them would find their way back into our cages. I know that because of the stains they'd still have on them from the berries. Why it never occurred to us that the gophers could dig out since the pen had a dirt floor I don't know. Lizard fights were something that we found pleasure in "hosting". We'd catch them and make them fight. We'd make dragonfly kites by easing up on the when they'd land and gently catch them by the tail. We'd tie a string to them and let the fly while we held the string. Who would have thought of such a thing! We'd let them go before too long though because we didn't want to hurt them. When Louie and Durrell got together they changed into daredevils. They'd catch anything! Charlotte would tell on them if they had a snake and Ma would force them to let it go. She never had to worry about me catching a snake but I wouldn't tell on the boys for doing it. Once the two of them caught a waft rat and thought it was "a pregnant opossum". Thank God someone realized what they had and killed it. They were going to "tend to it until the babies were born" Thank God he was looking out for them and kept them from getting bitten. It was strange that we didn't recognize it as a rat though since having a "rat killing" was a past time of ours too. We all had bb guns. We'd scout out the rats around the hog pens and shoot them. At an early age we were taught to respect guns of all types and how to use them safely. I liked the feel of the weapons but never really liked killing anything but I liked to practice on cans. I always had a nurturing side to me. I liked taking care of things. If an animal was deemed a "runt" or damaged in some way it was usually handed over to me. Many a bird's wing mended under my care. I even had bottles to feed the baby pigs that were labeled "runts". My dad managed to bring home odd things for me like baby squirrels or three legged chickens. He even had three hawks that he raised from chicks himself. The sad thing as they never did learn to provide for themselves. They would stay near our house in the trees and then they'd come to him and land on his arm for him to feed them. I guess we would have seemed like the Beverly Hillbillies if people got to know us. Like granny on the old show, Ma knew how to make lye soap. She made it to clean with. It worked better than anything on irons. The stench of the soap cooking could be smelled for miles away. She banked on using lye to fertilize her pecan trees too. She'd let us help. We'd dug a hole under the longest branch of the tree and we'd drop can and all into the hole. Later in the year we kids would dig it up just to see if the can was gone like she told us that it would be .We had to fertilize the trees when the sap was down and her trees never skipped a year of producing. Her pecan money was what she used as Christmas money. I never was a girly girl. As the tomboy that I was I felt most comfortable in jeans and a baseball cap. I did keep my hair long but most of the time it was tucked beneath a ball cap. More than once I was mistaken for a boy until I removed the cap and loosed the pile of hair that has hidden under it. My parents were no longer together. I wasn't allowed to see my mom so I had no one to teach me how to do girly things. Ma did try to instill simple things like the way a young lady should sit. She did not really possess the ability to teach me how to fix myself up. For goodness sake, she never even wore her teeth except to go to the doctor's office and even then it was just her top plate! It was a long time before I would become comfortable as a girl let alone a woman. I did have an aunt (Virginia) that tried to teach me proper etiquette. I remembered how beautiful my mother was. I never felt pretty myself. Compared to everyone else I thought I was awkward and plain. The girls in my class did not seem to have the problem that I did with their self esteem; so for the most part I kept to myself. As I grew into young adulthood I learned the art of disappearing. I learned how to fade into the background of others so that I would not be noticed. I would spend hours on end reading books. In the books I could be confident. The books did not care if I was plain. Like my mom, Aunt Virginia was a beautiful woman. She seemed to possess an aura that made her pretty no matter what she wore. No one I knew carried their self with the confidence that she did. She was often doing her nails and she even taught me how to do mine. She was comfortable with herself and I secretly longed to be like that. She had a daughter (Laura) that was losing her sight. Laura was pretty like her mom. She was no tomboy! Laura was proud to be a girl and even more proud to be growing into a woman. We all recall when she pulled up her shirt to show everyone that she was growing breast. She seemed to embrace her womanhood. She did not seem to have the companion of fear that often kept me company. She sang at her hometown functions with such confidence. She had great talent to sing and to act. I suppose that it was she that first gave me a love for plays. I listened to her quote things that at the time I had never heard and I was captivated. She has been an inspiration to me through the years. Losing her sight didn't stop her from doing anything! She prepared to go blind by learning Braille. She got the cane, the dog, the whole bit and still can cook for her family. I recall us having a piñata at a family reunion. All of the children tried to bust it. We all took turns then someone gave Laura the stick. I wondered if giving a girl almost blind a stick was a wise thing to do. As it turns out being "blindfolded" was not a handicap for her she was the one that busted open the piñata! Like I said earlier nothing seemed to stop her. She had learned to get around her disabilities and she never used them as an excuse for failure. So many times fear and/or what we consider our weaknesses stop us from trying to accomplish the things that we'd like to. Fear is not from God and yet for so much of my childhood it was my constant companion. I was afraid of things and/or people but my deepest fear rested within me. Because I was sexually abused I was afraid that evil was part of me and because I was bad somehow I had caused the abuse. It took me longer to forgive God and myself than it did to forgive the abusers. I wondered how God could allow this to happen to me as a child if he truly loved me. God gives people free will and he is not responsible for everything that people do. Somewhere in the healing process I felt that I heard my answer from the Lord. This is what I heard "Regina, I know that you have questioned why I let things happen to you and how could I just watch those things happen to you if I loved you. Where was I? I cannot look upon sin. I had to turn away when those things happened to you. It hurt me too much. I couldn't bear to watch. I didn't leave you during those times. I love you." I recall the exact words that the Lord spoke to me because of my journaling. He also led me to this scripture Habakkuk 1:13 thou art of purer eyes than to behold evil and canst not look on iniquity (or grievance). God speaks to us if we chose to recognize his voice. It sometimes comes as a feeling or thought that at first we may think is our own thoughts. If you pray for help to hear his voice he will teach you to hear. The act of forgiveness is an important part of the healing process. When all is said and done we have to forgive others for wrongs they've done to us. No matter how bad it was. If we can't forgive then we won't be forgiven. Forgiving others does not say the wrong done was nothing or that they deserve it. It releases us from the pain of the wrongs done to us. So many negative things had been spoken over me that I was afraid to allow myself to hope for better in my life. To live without hope is a sad way to exist. I was afraid to hope. Maybe that's one reason that it has taken me so long to share my book. We all have a story to share. There are things within us that are meant to be shared. Not every part of our story is to be shared some things are meant to be between God and ourselves. Wouldn't it be a waste to have things happen to us and not learn from those things? It is the through the things that happen in our lives that we learn and grow closer to God. There are so many of us that blame God and/or others for everything in our lives instead of taking any responsibility ourselves. It is true that things do happen to us that are beyond our control but it's how we respond to those things are our choice. I hungered for peace in my life. It always seemed to be just beyond my reach. It would take me many years to learn to rest in the peace of the Lord. My grandma had two large seashells on a dresser in her hallway. I loved those shells. I remember as a child sitting at the end of the hallway in the dark with one of those big shells rested against my little ear. In those shells I could hear what I thought peace would sound like if it could be heard. It sounded like the beach too. Before my parents divorced we got to go to the beach a lot but after the divorce we didn't get to go much. I missed the beach the sound of it and the smell of salt in the air. I missed my mom but I forced those feelings deep within myself. I missed things we did as a family like play cards or just hang out. Things were different now but not all bad. I pretended that I did not care about my mom because I thought it just made things easier for everyone. All feelings must be faced eventually no matter how deep we try to bury them. I would have a lot of hurts to overcome because of the feelings that I tried to bury. I had the misconception that it was best to be tough and not let anyone hurt me. I spent so much time learning the skill of becoming tough that I could no longer cry. When hurtful things happened to me I could sort of "hide within myself" and that is how I'd bare the abuse. I thought that if I didn't show emotion, then I was tough. When the emotional healing process began in my life and the tears started I feared that they'd never end. Maybe not allowing ourselves to cry is not such a good thing for us. In this life we all face hurt and disappointments. It is as if the tears release us from the pain of those hurts. If we dam up the tears then we hold onto the pain and we are unable to let things go. I liked to watch church on TV as a child because I rarely got to go. My daddy had been hurt by "church people" so he'd much rather take me fishing than to church. The more I pushed him to go to church with me the farther from church he got. He told me that church is like fishing "you keep what is good and throw the rest back". I did not care who was preaching I'd want to watch them. I remember watching a popular one on TV back then and my brother Louie hitting me on the head telling me I was "healed". He found the healing ministry funny but I took it in stride and kept watching. I had been baptized in 1985 at the Baptist church. My grandma told me that things were only going to get worse for me after I did that. I guess she knew that the devil was going to fight me even harder now. I was given a "Survival book" but no one tried to mentor me as a new Christian. I failed in a lot of areas. I had gotten discouraged from my mistakes plus getting a ride to church was causing conflict. My family thought I was going to church "too much" so for awhile I quit going. In 1988 a church was built close to my grandma's, it was so close that I could walk to it myself. A woman that was called a "prophet" was there for a few services. I had never heard of a prophet and I had never heard of anyone like her! This was no Baptist church but I did not care because I knew that what they had was real. All of my life I had been told stories about crazy things done in Pentecostal churches but I felt a peace there like no other I had known. This woman preacher came over to me during church and told me about a journal that I had kept hid. She went on to say that God himself saw my book and I would see all of the places that I longed to travel to. There was no way in the world that anyone could have told her about my writings because no one knew about it. She was right on the mark! She went on to say, "The man that you are going to marry, no-one is ever going to believe!" Well even a woman preacher can miss it sometimes I thought then because I knew my plan was to never marry but she did know about my book. More than that God knew about my book, which meant I was not insignificant to him after all. The funny thing is that when I tell people today who I married the first thing they say is "you married who?" just like she told me no one ever believes the man that I married. People have found us to be the most unlikely couple. I was prayed for in tongues. I had been taught that speaking in tongues weren't for today. Women in the church were around me as I was praying they prayed "in the spirit". It was nothing like I had thought. It wasn't scary at all in fact a sense of peace surrounded me. That night on the walk home I received the baptism in the Holy Ghost and began speaking in tongues. I seemed to receive it easily maybe because I hadn't been taught so much about it. Sometimes our education gets in our way of receiving things from God. I didn't really understand why I had received this precious gift or how to develop it at that time. What I did know was that it wasn't something I could share with my family at this point. So when I got home I managed to stop praying long enough to get past them to my room. I don't know how long I prayed before I stopped. My dad seemed to despise me going to church but I know now that it was my attitude about going that he disliked. I wanted everyone to experience what I was. The more I pushed them to go to church the more conflict we had .The Holy Spirit is who draws men to Christ not us. Sure we are to tell others about Christ and what he has done for us but we must allow the Holy Spirit to do the rest. We should live in such a way that it makes others want the relationship with God that we have. It wasn't only in the church building that I had this sense of peace. There was a Christian bookstore in Samson. I loved to go in there and just "soak up the atmosphere". The lady that owned the store was spirit filled only I did not know that at the time. I only knew that she played soft music and being in the store soothed my spirit. I'd look around and maybe get highlighters or a bookmark nothing expensive. I did not want to explain I just felt peace in there so I'd buy a little something when I went. Daddy didn't mind me going to the store at all. The bookstore lady was always kind to me. I have learned that I have that same peace resting inside of me now and I don't have to go anywhere to feel it. Sometimes we just need to tap into the things that God has already given to us. I have learned that for me shutting down the things of the world helps me to "be still and know that he is God". My Father gives us a peace that surpasses that of the world. It doesn't mean that this life will be a cakewalk. We all have had our family troubles. I moved out on my own when I was nineteen years old. I didn't leave on the best of terms. A few months before I moved out I had taken a nursing entrance exam with a friend of mine. I had no interest in becoming a nurse. My friend was afraid to go alone so she asked me to take the test "just for fun". I had no idea what I wanted to do with my life. As it would turn out she'd fail the test and I passed mine. I had worked at the junior college part time while I went. I had worked at a tomato packing plant and a pizza place. Then I got a job at the nursing home as a CNA. I was working at the nursing home when I got my first apartment. I wasn't making but three dollars and something an hour. My first apartment was everything that a first apartment should be. It was a small two-bedroom garage apartment. My mother and her husband Rodney helped me get it set up. I had contacted my mother before I moved out and this had caused some conflict. My place was made of block and it was simple to say the least. We decorated it with sparse furnishings. It was not things that I craved but peace and solitude. Rodney made sure that I had what I needed plus things I hadn't thought of. He got me a little space heater for my bathroom so I wouldn't be chilled when getting out of the shower. He was very thoughtful. He even hung a blind up in my bathroom just to humor me. The bathroom had a frosted window and no one could see in but it unnerved me to think of getting undressed for a shower with that window uncovered. He laughed but he hung the blind. My mother got me a table and dressed it up with the prettiest yellow tablecloth and place mats I'd ever seen. It was the little things that they did for me that meant the most. I was driven to the grocery store before they departed and they purchased the first of my supplies. The store was only a few blocks from my place and later I'd walk to get my groceries. I hesitated to choose things I didn't want to take advantage of their generosity. My mom loaded me up with things though to make sure I didn't starve until I could afford to buy myself some things. She seemed to think of everything from a can opener to Oreos. Now this was going to be the life I thought. I could sit up as late as I wanted and eat all of the Oreos I wanted. I didn't have a car. I had to walk everywhere. It turned out that the man I rented from was an assembly preacher. Mr. Hamilton told me I could ride to church with him and his family. They lived in the yard with me since my apartment was a garage apartment. The Hamilton family was good to me. It was just like God to provide the perfect place, right in a preacher's yard. I loved my new place. I walked to work rain or shine. I recall some of my co-workers helping me out when they'd see me walking different ones would pick me up and/or take me home sometimes. A particular co-worker would see me walking in the rain a time or two and she'd stop and yell, "Get in here! My God you are going to get struck by lightning!" More than once I found myself weighing out do I get in and hear the lecture or do I take my chances with the lightning? She still laughs about my "craziness" to this day. One thing people could say was that I was determined. I wanted to stand on my own two feet. As time passed by the reality of not making a lot of money and not having a car set in. I decided to call the nursing school where I took the entrance exam and just talk to them about the test. It had not been too long for me to get into nursing school and as it turned out the low income made it possible for me to get a Pell grant for school. The grant paid for all of my schooling but I still had to work to pay for my living expenses. Fear raised its ugly head. I knew people that had went to nursing school only to fail the board of nursing exam. I worried if I could do this or not. I was afraid of being humiliated but I decided to try even though I felt the odds were against me. I was offered a scholarship from work but declined it because if I failed boards I'd have to repay them the money and the Pell Grant had been free no matter what. Whispers came from my own mind at times telling me that this was too hard and that I couldn't do it. Fear of failure mocked me. My Uncle Milton had been through a divorce and was paying child-support. He was having a hard time himself so he moved in with me. He encouraged me when everything in me said to quit. He'd say corny things like I am betting on you and I don't bet on losing horses. I worked full-time as a CNA and went to nursing school full time. I went to school in the mornings then I would go in to work at 3pm and work until 11pm. I took no break between I actually would change into my work uniform at work in the bathroom. I was more tired than I ever had been. Often I fell asleep with books in my arms and my glasses on my face. I even recall falling asleep standing up in the shower once. I had many days throwing in the towel looked like it would be a relief. Uncle Milton was constantly saying "I bet on winners and you are a winner". I felt like anything but a winner but still I soldiered on. Somewhere during this time Uncle Milton started school himself at the same college. He took automotive classes. During his time at the school he ran into Marilyn, Mickey's sister. Milton learned that Mickey was in prison and he felt led to write him. We went to Marilyn's house and got his address. He proceeded to write him. After he had written him he asked me if I'd write to him and witness to him. I had always thought that this uncle of mine was crazy and now I knew it for sure, he was nuts! Here I was with almost no time between school and work to catch my breath, and he wants me to write a man in prison of all things! Did he think that I was crazy too? After all if I wanted a male friend they always seemed to be around. Men wanting a wife always seemed to be lurking around. By this time in my life I had came to the conclusion that marriage was not for me. I was content to have my own place and not have to fight with anyone. I had never seen many "good marriages" so I focused on my career. In our family the only couple other than my grandparents who had not been divorced was Uncle Louie and Aunt Ann. I did enjoy the attention that I got from the boys as long as they didn't get too close. I found myself thinking about writing to Mickey more and more in spite of myself. I decided to write him one letter to "witness" to him then his blood would not be on my hands. I wrote to him and explained who I was. I signed my letter as "Regina" the name all of my friend and family call me-not the name Janice that my workplace called me. I got stuck being called Janice at work because when I started I was timid. It's my first name so people referred to me by it and I just didn't speak up and correct them. I have ended up being called both names now. I joke about it though and tell people I had to have an alias just to marry Mickey. With my first letter to him mailed I focused harder on school and work. It was a relief to write him but I didn't know what kind of response he'd have. He'd probably think I was crazy for sure. Here I was I had written a man in prison. I had been taught that a girl was never to approach a boy without having been approached first. I had gone against my teachings just to send him a letter. I turned my attention toward my career because I was anxious about his response. I wasn't even sure he'd write me back. Within a little while I received my first letter from Mickey and instead of relief I felt intrigued. This man that wrote me was not what I had expected. There was a kindness in his words that seemed to beckon me to write again. I had longed for a true friend. A pen pal would be nice at this point I thought. Best of all he was in prison and he couldn't get close enough to hurt me, I thought. I was always careful to keep men at a safe distance. I had men trying to "get to know me" only I wouldn't let them close enough to see the real me. I'd go out to eat or just hang out with them but that's where it ended. Intimacy frightened me. For some reason on my rare "dates" thoughts of Mickey would creep into my mind. If only I could find someone like him that was interested in me, I thought; then I might let go of my staying single attitude. Mickey was older than me and always presented himself to me as a gentleman. I felt that he saw me as merely a friend. I'd embarrass both of us to hint at anything else. Looking back now I see that I was always drawn to him. As the years passed our letters grew closer and so did we. My "dates" with other men lessened. After getting to know Mickey the other men bored me. We had this connection somehow. He seemed to just "get me". I could share things with him that I chose not to share with anyone else. He seemed to understand me. To really know someone and have them know you started to be a comforting thought to me. There were a lot of things that we didn't share with each other. I dared not tell him that I feared I was falling in love with him, nor did I share the demons that rested in my mind. I felt that if I opened up to him completely that he wouldn't even want to be my friend. I chose my words to him wisely because I had began to rely on our friendship. I needed him like I needed air. His letters always seemed to give me a boost. I'd often find myself with this silly grin on my face after I got another letter from Mickey. The more he wrote the harder the other men seemed to pursue me. They'd give me all of the things that Mickey couldn't at this point. I received flowers, jewelry, and all sorts of gifts. Heck I even had one bring me produce like watermelons. Nothing they did lured me to them. I declined two marriage proposals. I liked both of the men okay. My heart was already taken and deep inside I knew it. Being with anyone except Mickey just did not feel right. It was him that I wanted only I couldn't tell him that. One suitor had taken me to the lake. That lake later had great significance to me. When I did get a truck of my own I took rides around the lake. During those rides alone I'd try to talk to myself and to God about Mickey. What I felt for him scared me. I tried to talk myself out of being in love with him and when that didn't work I concluded that I'd just have to keep him from finding out my feelings for him. At least with being his friend I was close to him, as close as I could ever be; I thought. How silly he'd think I was to admit my love for him when it seemed obvious that he saw me as his pen pal. During this time my dad sent me kiwi to my workplace through one of his many lady friends. We forgave each other and I went home to visit everyone. I liked being out on my own though and I didn't want to go back home to live .The time came for me to take my board test and I was scared. Mickey and Milton voiced their confidence in me if only I could feel confident. I took the test and returned to everyday life to wait 6 weeks for results. I went to work and learned that others had received results my Uncle Milton learned this too. He ran down the mail lady and got my envelope that contained my results. He brought it to my job and threw it behind the nurses' station in front of me. I was upset with him about this to begin with because I had pictured myself opening it in the privacy of my bathroom. Here I was with an audience to see my results. Everyone kept saying open it we love you no matter what. I couldn't open it myself so I handed it back to Milton and he opened it. "Congratulations!" was all he said. I passed it? He must have read it wrong. I snatched it from his hand to see for myself. Everyone was hugging me and telling me they knew I'd do it. Funny thing is I didn't believe it myself to begin with. My daddy was the first person I called when I passed my Board of nursing exam. He didn't outright say he was proud of me but I sensed he was when he told me I needed to go on back to school and further my nursing career. His confidence in me seemed to have grown. Next I called my mom and Rodney. I talked nonstop for hours to anybody that would listen. The first thing I done was bought me a new Ford Ranger truck. By letter, Mickey told me how proud he was of me. When I got his letter I took another drive around the lake. I weighed out telling him the truth about my feelings for him but fear of losing his friendship stopped me. My brother Louie came by my apartment a few times to visit. He even once came by after a party and asked me to take his friends and him home because they'd had too much to drink. I was glad he did that and had not tried to drive himself home. I let him know I was still there for him even though I no longer lived at home. My uncle Milton still lived with me because his financial situation was still not good. We moved a couple of times looking for cheaper places to stay. At one place, he had a barn where he raised rats and mice for snake people to supplement his income. Plus he liked doing it as a hobby. He liked crazy animals he caught me a baby raccoon and I attempted to make a pet out of it but I think it was too old when I got it. He had a friend that brought us a wild bobcat to nurse back to health. We got a permit for it and housed its cage in our back room of the rented house. You'd think a snarling bobcat would slow down suitors. I finally began distancing myself from the men wanting to date me. We had a friend who had a pet store in her house. We'd go by and help her when we could sometimes. She was an insightful old lady and I enjoyed her company. I found a nicer house in Kinston. We moved into it. It was huge I even had a room for weights and exercise equipment. So I had my own gym. My brother Louie had finally "settled down". He was married and even had a son, Michael. I remembered walking to the playground near my first apartment and watching the children play. I didn't think I'd ever marry and I felt ill equipped to have children of my own. Secretly though I wondered what it would be like to have a child myself, and somewhere deep inside I had longed for one. Michael seemed to satisfy this longing and kept it quite within me. Mickey told me he'd like to call me if I got a phone. The nursing home knew where I lived so they'd sent police for me when they wanted me to go in to work on my days off. I reasoned that if I got a phone they could just call me plus

Mickey could call. I imagined what it would be like to hear his voice instead of reading a letter. I worked a lot but I was content. Everything was right again in my world and I had no way of knowing that once again my world was about to shift. While at work, I got a phone call from my daddy's lady friend. She told me to "stay calm" my brother Louie had been in an explosion at work but she didn't know where he was or if he was okay". I don't remember who I gave my med keys to or who was working with me that day. I managed to call my Uncle Milton. He told me to swing by and get him that Louie was probably taken to Enterprise hospital since that was closest to his work place. Thank God he was able to think clearly. We raced to the hospital. When I arrived family was in the ER waiting area and someone told me a pressure cooker exploded and Louie had been burned. Everyone then just stood there quietly looking at me I heard myself yell, "Where is he? Is he okay?" Daddy told me he "wasn't that bad and they had just flew him to Birmingham". Oh my God! They don't fly people to Birmingham if they aren't that bad. I called mom and told her about the accident. Milton drove me to Birmingham. It was as if we crawled there. I prayed and cried all the way. Memories of him bringing chili that he'd cooked to my house and memories of our childhood competed for a place in my mind. It was if I was in a fog and all of my thoughts were unclear. Somewhere in my jumbled thoughts I thought of Mickey. If only I could talk to him I knew I could calm down. I longed to talk to him but there was no time to think of him right now. We finally made it to UAB (the hospital). We had some difficulty locating Louie because of the layout and size of the hospital. Finally, we found him! He was in the critical care unit. A nurse attempted to prepare me for seeing Louie. There was no way to prepare me to see my brother like this. We were told the next couple of days were "touch and go". He had been burned pretty badly. 65% of his body was burned the worst burns were third and forth degree. I took a deep breath and walked into the unit. I will never forget the smell even now it is branded within my mind. Louie had a lot of equipment attached to him. He had a catheter, a large tube in his nose, electronic blood pressure monitor, o2 sat monitors, IVS. It was hard to tell which one he was. All of the patients in the unit looked alike because of the swelling and the shaved heads. Louie's black hair was replaced with a bald one. Many scenes from our lives flashed before me. A nurse directed me to his bed. I found the strength to step closer to him and touch his hand. He woke and asked, "What are you doing here?" I choked back tears and said where else would I be? He tried to talk more but it was hard for him. I told him to rest and reassured him I would be here at the hospital for as long as he needed me to be and I'd visit as often as they'd let me. During my stay at UAB I saw several patents "go bad" in the unit. Many of them died. When they'd bring one out I'd hold my breath and pray that it wasn't my brother. I know that it seems selfish but that is what I did. He was stuck so much that they had to do a "cut down" just to have access to a vein. More family showed up in the days that came. I returned to work when he was deemed "stable" but I returned on days off and stayed as long as I could. Often I spent the night by his bed when he was moved out of the unit into a room. When I stayed his wife took a break. During this time I had written Mickey about the accident and I poured my heart out to him. He'd call to check on Louie and me. He'd tell me sometimes that he didn't know what to say but he'd listen. It was good to hear him on the phone and I was glad that I had gotten a phone. Just knowing someone really heard me seemed to ease my mind. He never tried to tell me what I should or shouldn't feel. He just listened when I needed him the most. All of our childhood I tried to protect my brother and once again I was unable to do so. Louie confided in me during his stay at the hospital. He told me he was ashamed that he screamed when he was in the tank but went on to say that everyone did. The tank was part of his treatment. The nurses took burn patients there to "scrub the damaged skin off of them". I advised him to scream as loud as he wanted to. There was no shame in it. The morphine he was given prior to going down to the tank did not help the pain. I would pray with him before he went and while he was gone. Then he started asking me to pray. In my mind I compared the tank to hell. The smell and the constant screaming in those scrubbing tanks must be like what it would be like there with the torment and no comfort to be found. There were some nights that I couldn't sleep. I'd sit by his bed and watch his oxygen levels and make sure that his breathing was okay. In desperation I'd read my bible out loud. Even as he slept I knew that his spirit heard the word. What I didn't realize was that his roommate found comfort in my reading. He ended up asking me to bring him a bible, which we did. His story was a sad one. He was having marriage problems and his wife turned on the gas stove and let fumes fill their home. She knew his habits. He was a smoker. She took their daughter and left him. He walked into his home not knowing where she was with a lit cigarette in his mouth. The house blew up around him. How he got out no one knows. He was burnt worse than my brother and it was no accident. He could not use his hands. Often he'd ask me to read more or to give him a sip of water while I was there. Once when the roommate was in the tank Louie told me his story. He'd fill me in while his roommate was gone for his treatments. During one of our talks Louie told me that the roommates wife had came and she brought divorce papers and threw them on his bed and left. Louie said man, how cold is she? He wouldn't even be here if it weren't for her and the man can't sign the papers anyways because he can't use his hands. I often wonder what ended up happening to him. I can only hope that he has recovered somewhat and has come to know Christ. Louie's accident was at work. He jumped down from a pressure cooker while being burnt and managed to find a hole in a wall to escape through. If it had not been for the hole he would have been killed. That's just like God. He makes us a way to escape. He told me that he showered down at work to try and get cooled down and to get the chicken off of him. His vision was temporarily impaired so he was unable to see if what he was washing off was chicken or his own skin. Louie made it through the burn center alive. I know that his life was spared for a reason. I witnessed him going through this and I am pretty sure that he would agree that there are no words adequate to describe the experience. I still pray for him because he is my brother and I love him. Mickey was released from prison some time after I passed boards. I already had deep feelings for him and yet I had no idea what he currently looked like. A lot of people would find that crazy. It's true though. I got to know him from the inside out. I had seen him years earlier and I had saw pictures at Marilyn's when Milton first got his address. I was still working three to eleven at the nursing home. Mickey's dad (Grady) visited a lady friend of his there. Grady and I became friends before he learned that I was writing to Mickey. I did not even know Mickey had been released and I was about my every day business. He came strutting in and asked for me by name. I recall glancing up from the nurse's station and seeing him. It hadn't occurred to me that this was Mickey. I got up and walked down the hallway with him just enough to get away from the peering eyes of my curious co-workers. I reasoned that he was a family member of one of my patients but he was looking good. I asked him how I could help him and he looked puzzled for a minute then he realized I didn't recognize him. He stammered out yeah maybe you can then just stood there. Finally I said look do I know you? He laughed and replied yeah you should we've been writing each other for years. Then he smiled one of the biggest smiles I've ever seen. Here was the man of my dreams standing before me in jeans and cowboy boots. We hugged and exchanged brief hellos. Out of the corner of my eye I saw a co-worker checking him out. I did not like that too much so I walked further down the hall with him. There was a door at the end of the hall and he thought I was walking him out the door. What I didn't realize is he had been drinking a little. I invited him to come back and have coffee with me after my shift. He misunderstood me walking him to the door and inviting him for "coffee" since he had drank a drink or two. He did give me his number before he left. I hoped he came back but at 11pm –he wasn't there. Well he had to have me pointed out to him too so I thought he didn't like my looks .I took this as further proof that he wasn't interested in me as more than a friend. What a shame I thought because he was nice looking to boot. I had his number and I was afraid to call him. Over the next months I'd find myself with his number in my hand. I hadn't received any calls from him or any letters since he was "home". I missed his letters. I really missed him and yet I wandered how that can be. You can't miss what you've never had, can you? I'd resolve to call then I'd hang up before anyone could answer. I admit it I was chicken. I just didn't think I could stand it if a woman answered his phone. I was no fool and Mickey was no priest. I had heard of his reputation with the women from my childhood. During my teenage years, I walked down to a friend's home to buy Avon. Before leaving her house she causally said, "Mickey doesn't like your hair cut". I asked her Mickey who? Exasperated she replied "well Mickey Moody of course!" It was one of the first times I actually recall hearing his name. I went home and asked daddy who Mickey Moody was. He flipped out on me and asked where did you hear that name? He went on to tell me to stay away from him. His family is so mean that if they can't find someone to fight they fight each other. I smiled thinking back on the boxing gloves they had gotten us to let us fight. During the years that came I would hear bits and pieces about things that Mickey had supposedly done. My dad had a little run in with the law himself and managed to get himself arrested on Ma's front porch for DUI. He had his day in court. He came home telling us that he" had just witnessed Mickey defending himself in court and that he made them look like fools in their own courtroom!" He was smart daddy said and I could tell he was impressed but then he added he's still a dangerous man though so you keep away from him. All of these memories would aide in my postponing writing to him in years to come. As Mickey's luck seemed to go once again he had gotten himself arrested. Grady came by the nursing home for his visit with his friend and he told me. He's back in jail! He got into trouble with that live-in girl friend he had. She'd had him arrested, which meant that he had violated parole. It was near Thanksgiving so I asked Grady if he was going to take him a plate. He said, "No, I ain't even going to see him he got himself in and so he can get himself out." It was more than my heart could bare. Here he was back in trouble and alone. I called information and got the number for the jail. Before I left work that day I called and found out when visiting was. I asked them to tell Mickey that Regina was coming to visit on visiting day. What they ended up telling him was "your girlfriend will be here on visiting day". He didn't want to see her after all in his mind she was the reason that he was there. The next few days crawled along but finally visiting day came. I went to the jail. I made sure that my makeup was just right but I wore nothing too dressy just jeans a simple blouse. I signed the list and waited to go back to visit. I had asked my Uncle to come along. After all I was a lady. I approached the metal door with the little window. The others in there saw me and started trying to coax Mickey to visit with me. He still didn't understand I was there. He thought it was the girlfriend. After several minutes I heard one of them say, "well if you ain't going to visit her I am." He got up and looked through the window and realized it was me. He laughed and told me man they told me my girlfriend was out here. I had difficulty hearing him through the glass window. There were holes in the metal door. The phone on the door did not work. You had to speak through the holes and then turn your head to listen through them when spoken to. I managed to find a piece of paper in my purse and I jotted him a note that said I would always be there for him no matter what I was his friend and I promised him that he would never be alone. I slid the paper through a crack in the door. He saved the note. I didn't understand any of this. The butterflies that bolted through my stomach that day I saw him at the nursing home were back and were just as active in my stomach now as they were then. Still we continued to tell everyone and ourselves that we were "just friends". Our letters started back. We vowed we'd stay friends no matter what. I felt bad for him but I had my friend back if only by default. I was thankful to have him in my life in whatever way that I could. I cherished every letter I received. On another day, Uncle Milton and I were having a burger at the Grill in Geneva. My burger suddenly became hard to swallow. I found myself thinking of Mickey having to eat jail food. Milton sensed something was wrong and asked me what I was thinking. I told him that I was just wishing Mickey could have a burger he didn't even look up from his but he said so order him one and we'll take it to him. While we were waiting on Mickey's burger a man overheard my dilemma. He told us he was an ex-preacher himself. Then he told me "girl, don't waste your time Mickey's hopeless and you'd better learn that you can't save them all". I was outraged by his words but I didn't bother to respond. Some people just don't understand God's grace. The man did say he was an ex-preacher and with this attitude it was no wonder he was no longer in ministry. I secretly hoped one day this same man would run up on Mickey and he'd witness to the man. That would be great and like the God that I serve to do something like that just to show him that no one is hopeless unless God says he is. God has the power to rescue anyone who wants to be saved. We managed to get the burger approved for Mickey, which was a miracle within itself and then they let us visit with him while we were there. This visit was different than before I got to see him through the bars of a cell not through a small window. We could both see and hear each other. It felt strange but good. It felt too good on my part. When our eyes met there was something there that forced me to turn away from them. In Mickey's eyes I seemed to see what I felt myself. It was in that very minute that I knew we were kindred souls. I was imprisoned by things too and was more like him than anyone realized. I gladly let Milton ramble on but I can't recall a single word that he said to Mickey. Our visit came to an end. We walked out into the fresh air and as I crank my truck, I knew that I was leaving a part of me there in that jail. Mickey was soon moved to Atmore prison. Our visits were not often and yet I felt drawn to him. He seemed to be one of the strongest men I'd ever known. Our "friendship" continued to grow. Uncle Milton rode with me to visit him at Atmore a few times because I still keep up the pretense that I thought of him as my friend. The first time visiting in Atmore prison was different from the jail. It was something else! We had to get "clearance" into the prison. This was no jail! I recall having to be frisked before I could see him. The woman doing it seemed to enjoy her job more than I was enjoying the procedure. I was thankful that I got to keep my clothes on .I shared my thoughts about it with Mickey and he laughed. I wasn't sure I could come back and go through that again. I later found out she was dismissed for getting too personal during the frisking and I was relieved. I did end up going back. The visiting room was dully painted, gray. It looked pretty much like a cafeteria. There were tables everywhere and Mickey got to sit at a table with us. It was nice just to be near him. I could hear him clearly and see him too. It was a hassle to get in to visit but it was worth it for me once he walked into the room. During the visit a little red headed boy caught my attention. He was visiting his dad. I thought of that image in years to come. His face tugged at my heart. I thought it was sad that he had to see his dad here but his laughter filled the room despite the gray walls. Mickey smoked Marlboro's back then and we could buy them for him to smoke while we visited. The thing that I remembered most was the milk. He always drank a lot of milk during our visits. He admitted that he didn't get "real milk" except when I visited. It was usually powered milk. Being a milk drinker myself I understood why he had such a thirst for the real thing. What I couldn't understand was why in the months to come I had problems drinking my milk. I'd pour myself a cold glass and as I was trying to drink it, I felt like my throat itself closed up. I'd end up pouring it out. I know it seemed silly but I was madly in love with Mickey by this time. The hook had been set and no matter how I wiggled I couldn't get free of him. I tried to deny it to myself and I certainly didn't confess it to him or anyone else. If you truly love someone you care about what they are going through as if you are going through it yourself. Unbeknown to me Mickey was fighting his feelings for me. He was thinking about our age difference and he says he had no idea how I felt about him. I did try to keep my feelings about him hidden. Once during a visit, I let my guard down without thinking. We were all going outside to take a picture Uncle Milton was leading the way. I reached for Mickey's hand without thinking. He was so shocked that he hesitated to take my hand so I thought he hadn't noticed. I was relieved and dropped my hand quickly telling myself that with another mistake like that I'd let the cat out of the bag. Mickey kept his feelings hid well too so I had no idea of his battle. When we all got outside for some reason my Uncle Milton decided he didn't want to be in the picture and he said "ya'll go ahead". Mickey threw his arm around me and we posed for the picture together. No matter how we fought it something always seemed to be pushing us together. I smiled for the camera and tried my best not to melt right there in front of everyone. The feel of his arm around me felt natural like it belonged there. Minutes before, I had almost made a fool of myself reaching for him and yet here he was with his arm around me. It seemed to me like the picture was snapped too soon as I liked the feel of his arm around me. The "ice queen" was melting. I had been called that several years ago by a boyfriend basically because I had refused to sleep with him. I didn't mind the title though because the truth was I felt I had earned it. When you go years without crying you tend to grow cold. I welcomed the coldness. I thought that in the security of it I was "safe". No one could get close enough to really hurt me. That place was my prison. The walls that secured me within them were as strong and solid as the walls of any prison. It was a place of darkness and loneliness. I told myself that I was content. I had a good job and had done well for myself. Happiness and contentment are not the same. I thought that I had things "as good as it ever could be for me". Fear of getting hurt causes you to close your heart. A closed heart is the worse type of prison that there is. My heart had been sealed up for a long time. I didn't know how it happened but it seemed that Mickey held the secrets to unlocking my heart. Deep down I knew that this man could really hurt me but I promised myself I'd be careful. He made me a jewelry box that looked like a gazebo. It had hearts hand carved on it, secret compartments, swinging doors and even a swing. It must have taken him a long time to make it. I held it all the way home and let Milton drive. It was of great value to me. It was the first thing handmade he'd given me other than the cards. My dad saw the gift while visiting me. He asked me where I had gotten it as he stood admiring it. I confessed that Mickey had made it for me. I down played my feelings for him yet again. I told daddy that we'd been writing one another for a few years and that we had became friends. Daddy didn't say much more about the gift or about my friendship with Mickey. Mickey was struggling with his feelings for me but at this point I had no idea. There were things about him that I would learn later. While he was in the jail in Geneva awaiting transfer (to Atmore) he found himself in turmoil. He must have been disgusted with women at this point. There was what he referred to as a jailhouse prophet in there with him. The "prophet" told Mickey that he would have a godly woman in his life. He even had gone as far as to tell Mickey that her name would be Janice. As I shared earlier I use both of my names (Janice and Regina). For years Mickey recognized me as Regina. He didn't know my first name in the beginning. In the meantime, a woman named Janice had come upon his path and had even wanted the two of them to marry. He wrote me about it. I didn't know about the "prophesy", and I advised him to marry her if he was in love with her. He wrote me back still not telling me about the "prophesy" but he hinted that for some reason he didn't trust this Janice. I wasted no time in responding. I secretly didn't want him to marry her anyways but fear hushed me. I told him how important it was that he trusts the woman he was going to marry. I went on to say that if he didn't trust her he shouldn't marry her. I mailed my advice and I prayed he wouldn't marry her. He'd told me that even if he married her "she wouldn't come between his and my friendship". I don't know why I didn't tell him the truth about why I didn't want him to marry her. I felt that I had betrayed his friendship in a sense by deceiving him. Well I eased my conscious by reasoning that anyone considering marriage should trust who they were about to marry. Just the mere mention of him with another woman caused my heart to ache. The fear of losing him threatened me. He backed out of the marriage and wrote me to tell me. When I received the letter I admit I was relieved. I realize now that the devil was trying to stop us from being together even then. God had a plan for us. I didn't recognize the importance of my name to Mickey. Remember he still had not shared the words the prophet spoke to him. For some reason, after years of writing him; I mistakenly signed my first name to one of my letters to him. He called and questioned me about my name Janice. Why hadn't I told him my first name was Janice? I did not understand what the big deal was. I told him that his daddy called me Janice because he met me at the nursing home. People that I work with knew me as Janice. I liked my friends to call me Regina like my family did. In Mickey's mind my name was significant. He believed the prophet on some level that is why he'd considered marrying the other Janice. When her true colors came out he knew she wasn't from God. He was confused. What did the prophecy mean now? Could it be that maybe I was to be the woman God put with him? Wasn't I "his friend"? He searched his own feelings and questioned mine within the boundaries of his mind. He kept quiet about the words the prophet had spoken over him. He pondered its meaning in his heart. He was coming up for parole again. Milton and I did what we could to help him. I prayed for his release. When I got the phone call telling me he was getting out I was excited for him and scared for me. In my mind's eye I begin to see what it had been like before. I was afraid I was once again about to lose my friend. How selfish is that? I had rather him be locked away than lose him? I took another ride around the lake. I knew he was not a man that would be comfortable with living a celibate life. He'd soon find another woman and he'd forget all about me. In spite of all of my fears I was happy for him. He'd be free. If I really cared about him I should be happy about that. I prepared myself to really "set him free". I knew the saying about if you set something free and it comes back to you...I really believed though that once he was out he'd stop writing me again. I'd promised him that I would pick him up the day that he was released. I determined in my mind to make that a happy day. I wanted to do something with him so I'd have a day to recall having spent with him. I had hungered for time with him so I planned to make that most of the day. I planned to look as good as possible when I picked him up but I didn't want to appear to be dressed up. My nerves were getting the best of me. I went to extra tanning sessions. I purchased a pair of cotton navy blue shorts and I pretty white blouse. The blouse had a satin feel and the sleeves reminded me of a matador for some reason. The cut of the blouse was perfect it fit me snug but didn't reveal more than my shape. I didn't want to look trashy. I chose my simple white canvas shoes to complete my causal look. It was August just before my twenty-fifth birthday when he was released. It was hot and I wanted to appear relaxed as if this was just any summer day. There had been delays with his release day because of paperwork. Relaxed was not the best word to describe me. The days dragged along and my excitement soared. Finally I got the call to tell me when I could pick him up. Being a proper southern lady I knew I shouldn't pick him alone. I asked Uncle Milton to ride with me to get him. The morning of Mickey's release I handed over my truck keys to Milton. I was much too nervous to drive but I tried to act as if this was no big deal. When we arrived at the prison I went inside to find Mickey. I had to wait for a few minutes for him to be called. While I waited several inmates came by and smiled at me. I secretly hoped I looked okay. When Mickey walked in his smile lit up the room. Others inmates smiled at him and wished him well as we left the building together. Milton and Mickey shook hands and greeted one another. Mickey asked Milton if he could place his things in the back of the truck and explained that he had a surprise in his belongings for my upcoming birthday. Once his things were secured, we pulled out of the parking lot. Milton had resumed the driving. I sat in the middle but closer to Mickey so I didn't have to straddle the gear shift. Acting "cool" was difficult for me to do with my legs touching Mickey's. He seemed at ease so I tried to keep up the pretense. The three of us talked a lot. We planned to eat at Golden Corral. Milton wanted us to have a "good steak". Mickey was telling Milton about "my birthday surprise". I tried to focus on his words but fire seemed to be surging through my leg that was still touching his. Milton was rambling on and all I could do was sit there thinking these ungodly thoughts of Mickey. I knew I'd had to repent long and hard about these thoughts as well as what I was feeling. Mickey smiled down at me as if he could read my thoughts. For just a split second I wondered if he felt it too. Was the same fire blazing through him? Our meal was nice. During casual conversation Milton mentioned the beach that I liked to go to. I had sent Mickey pictures of it in one of my letters and told him about the seclusion of it. Before I knew it Milton suggested that we all ride down to the beach after all we were celebrating! Mickey said he'd love to go but did not have anything fit to swim in. I told him that I wanted to get him a late birthday present since he had mine in the truck. Something to swim in would be just the ticket! He agreed to let me buy him the outfit. I would have done anything at this point just to spend more time with him. In the back of my mind something whispered you'd better make the most of this day it'll probably be the last you see him. When we got to the store Milton helped him pick out a pair of shorts and a tee shirt to match it. There had been a man that visited the nursing home who wanted to marry me.

He wore yellow shorts most of the time. He wore them so often to visit that a co-worker would tease me and say, "has ole yellow been to see you yet today"? Milton had known about the man. He suggested that Mickey try on a yellow pair of shorts. He agreed to just because Milton insisted that I was "crazy about yellow". When Mickey emerged from the dressing room sporting the yellow outfit I knew he had fallen for Milton's prank. Much to his pleasure Milton smiled at me and I smiled back. Neither of us told Mickey that I didn't really like yellow that much. The funny thing is on Mickey anything looked good to me. Milton grinned as the saleslady placed the yellow clothes into a bag and handed then to Mickey. He learned on our honeymoon about the joke and he vowed to get even with Milton. We stopped by our house and I put on a bathing suit under my shorts. I was nervous about Mickey seeing me in my bathing suit but I wasn't ready to let go of him just yet. No matter how I lied to myself, nothing had protected my heart from losing him. We all enjoyed the beach. We laugh now thinking of me picking up a man that had been in prison and showing him my black two-piece bathing suit. It wasn't a bikini it was tastefully cut. Mickey jokes and tells people that I know how to catch a man. We made a whole day of it together. After the beach we went through a fast food place. We took our burgers to a gazebo and had ourselves a picnic. I really enjoyed this day and I hoped that Mickey had. As I climbed into bed that night my heart sank. I thought I would never see him again or at least not anytime soon. He would be going on his merry way and somehow I reasoned with my heart that I would have to live through this. I ached to tell him how I felt but I knew that I couldn't. I had not set out to fall in love with him but somewhere along the way I had. I managed to keep it a secret. I was afraid to tell Mickey. I imagined how he'd probably laugh at the thought that I might could think he'd love me back. Once you feel rejection you never forget it and you don't want to risk it happening again. The next morning I scolded myself again for letting myself fall so hard for a man that I could not have and I took another drive around the lake. I knew that I had to face reality. The thing is reality is not always what it seems. Sometimes it hides its face. I came home from work one afternoon and I couldn't believe my eyes! My yard looked like a different place the shrubs where cut and the flowers were trimmed back. Mickey was still at it when I pulled into the carport. I asked him what he was doing. He told me that he wanted to do something to thank me for all I had done for him. I learned that he'd worked all day in my yard. Over the next few months I saw him almost every day. He'd go to church with me or just come by my house and hang out. He always left by ten though and was a perfect gentleman towards me. Heck he never even kissed me until one week before we got married. Even then it was me that kissed him good night. I will never forget the look of shock that came onto his face that night. Finally a weekend came when I didn't see him or hear from him at all. Again I scolded my foolish heart because by now I was thinking just maybe he did have feelings for me too. After that weekend, I couldn't stand it another minute so I decided to pack and head out to Orlando to visit a friend. Before I could start packing the phone rang. Mickey's daddy called me and told me that he had left his house pretty upset. He begged me to "find him and talk to him". I had no idea where he could be but he had left walking Grady said so he couldn't be far. The strange thing I learned later he was thinking of heading to Orlando himself. He told me that as he was walking he saw a rusty ½ inch or 9/16th wrench in the road and he heard the Lord say tighten up and be a man. I was looking through my purse for car keys and trying to explain to Milton what Grady had said when the phone rang. It was Mickey on the phone and he sounded like he was crying. He wouldn't talk to me he asked for Milton to come and get him from the store on highway 52 so he did so without me since Mickey wouldn't tell me what was wrong. Fear of receiving love causes people to push others away. I don't recall where he and Milton went or what happened next but I do recall that over the next few days' things in our lives started falling into place. We both had hit a wall of our own making. We knew that we belonged together. One day on my many rides around the lake I had a vision. I had never had this happen before and to be honest I wasn't sure what to make of it. I was close to God and often while riding around the lake I would sing and/or have praise music playing. The vision was as if I was watching it on a movie screen. It was that clear to me. It was confusing to me because of what I saw and how I saw it. I saw Mickey and myself on some sort of stage. It looked like an auditorium of some sort. In the vision Mickey was speaking and I was with him standing behind him. A large crowd of people were gathered around listening to him speak. As he spoke they started laying things down on the "stage" floor. At that time I thought the things they were placing on the floor was strange. I recall seeing dollar bills, mirrors straws, pipes, and all other type of things people used to do drugs with. At that time I really didn't understand everything that I did see placed before me. God doesn't always show us the whole journey that we will have to go through before our visions/prophesies are fulfilled. One day on my ride home from work I spotted Mickey walking from Opp toward the town we lived in. I slowed my truck as I approached him. As cool as I could, I asked "do you want a ride?" He thanked me and stepped into the truck. He placed his bag of groceries between us on the seat and began lecturing me about the dangers of picking people up. I smiled and said "so do you want to get out?" I continued to drive and he smiled back. Quietness fell between us for a few moments. All of a sudden he raised his voice just a bit and said "do you know what's wrong with you? You need to be married." To which I laughed. Nothing else was said between us until I dropped him off safely at his dads. Sometime later Milton suggested the three of us go back to the beach. This time we took a raft. Mickey pulled me around the water on the raft. I recall the way Mickey looked. His hair was wet and tousled. I knew I had never been more attracted to him than I was at that moment. We chatted and I heard the echo of people around us talking and laughing. We were laughing too. Then as if on cue silence fell over the people and I heard nothing but the salty waves splashing against the raft. If there was ever a perfect moment in my mind this was it. Mickey proposed to me in that moment. He didn't just ask me to marry him and leave it at that. He explained the pros and cons of marrying him to me and then he allowed me time to think about it. How could he have known I had dreamed of it for years? That was only fantasy but marrying him in reality did scare me a little. I couldn't believe my ears Mickey Moody had really proposed to me! We had both considered our age difference and difficulties that we'd have to face. I did take a few days to mull it over because as much as I loved him the thought of marrying anyone scared me. All of my life I vowed I'd never get married and here I was considering it. I couldn't eat or sleep. I tried to imagine my life without him but I couldn't bare the thought of being without him. I knew somewhere deep inside my heart that living without him would only be existing. When I was by his side I felt like I had everything. Mickey wanted an answer but he was patient with me. He told me at some point that we wanted me to be happy. He went on to say he wanted me to think about what I wanted. He challenged me to not consider what anyone else wanted, not even him. He asked me to answer with what I wanted. If the answer was no he could deal with that but he wanted me to think about what I wanted and answer to the desires on my heart. It was as if my feelings really mattered to him. For the first time in my life I met with a man that put my feelings above his own. I threw caution to the wind and agreed to be his bride. We started out by telling our families. Uncle Milton was upset about it. My brother said "I always said you'd need a strong man or you'd run over him but I didn't mean this strong!" but he hugged me and congratulated us. His dad was thrilled! He had been telling Mickey that I was the woman for him. He had even lied to other women that had been calling for Mickey. He wanted to "help us along". He told them he was already with someone else. Mr. Grady was a rascal but he knew that I was truly in love with his boy. He knew it before Mickey did. He'd saw the evidence of it. Thrilled was not the word I would use to describe my daddy's reaction. He resolved to walk me down the aisle and give me away, "if that's what I really wanted him to do". We had taken him out to eat to tell him because we thought that he'd maybe behave better in a public place. We told my mom by going to her work place (a jewelry store. We strolled in hand in hand. She greeted us and asked what are ya'll up to today? We said, "We are here to pick out rings." Then both of us peered into the glass display case as if we were mere customers. She ran around the glass counters and hugged us both. We did pick out our rings there that day. Mickey insisted that I have more than a simple band. Diamonds is what he kept saying to me. My ring caught his eye and he asked my mom to get it out. I looked at the price. He was laying bricks for a living. I thought that ring was beyond our reach since our wedding would be three weeks away. When we decided we wanted each other as man and wife we saw no need in delaying it much longer. After all in our hearts we'd delayed enough. My mom said, "That's not your price Regina, you get the family discount" but even with that it would be a stretch. Mickey did not seem concerned about the price too much all he knew is "that is your ring". The owner of the store heard our dilemma. He motioned for Mickey to come in the back of the store with him. The two of them spoke and Mickey came out with an even lower price-to which neither of us could believe for both of our rings. He had chosen a nugget type ring for him to compliment mine. We proudly placed our rings on layaway. I couldn't believe that I was going to have such a nice wedding ring at such a discounted price. It seemed like everything we needed for the wedding had started falling into place. We went to a park after we got our rings ordered. There was a gazebo there. Mickey sat down on the steps of it and beckoned me to sit in front of him. He put his arms around me and we talked more about our upcoming wedding. We sat there for a while just laying plans for our lives together. It was as if I was in a fairy tale and for a change I was the princess. Mickey had this way of making me feel things I had never felt before. Three weeks was not a long time to throw together a wedding but when God ordains something he blesses it and makes a way. Looking back now, I think people may have thought I was pregnant. We did seem to want to do it quickly. We wanted our wedding simple and no debt. I borrowed my dress. Like all traditional brides, I wouldn't let Mickey see my dress. I wanted to surprise him when he saw me in it on our wedding day. We did all of the necessary things we had to do and even attended several hours of pre-marriage counseling. Our wedding turned out to be beautiful. It was simple but it was and still is a good memory for me. My daddy walked me down the aisle. He did tell me that he could just as easily walk me out the back door if I had changed my mind (before the wedding). He saw that this was what I wanted so he made peace with it. I promised him if he'd walk with me this once he'd never have to do it again. He joked and said you'd better listen to the wedding march it says "dum,dum,dum, dum." When I think back to that day I can still see Mickey waiting for me in the front of the church. The moment that our eyes met it was as if no one was there except the two of us. I recall someone straightening the train to my dress and opening the double glass doors for my entrance. I felt like a princess that day. My prince awaited me at the altar. The wedding was beautiful. We went on a short honeymoon. It was a weekend at the beach but it was a good beginning for the life that lay before us together. We had been attending church together. I was happier than I had ever been. Everything seemed almost too perfect in fact. The first year of marriage usually has adjustments. A couple of weeks after we were married we went to game room downtown in Samson. I was never allowed in "game rooms" as a girl. I found that not only did my husband have a talent to play pool but also I liked to watch him play. Out the front window I saw several police cars pulling up. Mickey said, "They must be after me bringing so many cars" He was joking but it turned out that they were there for him because of an old fine. I couldn't believe it two weeks after we were married and I had to follow them and watch him be "booked" then they allowed me to sign his bond. During the weeks that followed he bought himself a pool stick and started taking me with him a little to places where he could shoot pool. Mickey was late coming home from work one day nightfall had arrived and no word from him. I paced the floor and the yard until finally I saw the truck lights turn into the drive. He had been drinking. This was not the Mickey that I knew. I did not realize until much later in our marriage that there were snares that had been laid for him before we got married. Many things had come against him at that time that I did not understand. Still I loved my Mickey. I tried to accept him as he was and he did the same for me but still it was not always easy. Two months after we were married I got sick. The sickness seemed to come and go. I warned Mickey to keep his distance because I didn't want him to catch this "flu". He laughed and said yeah, you got the flu all right. After about a week of the sickness going away and returning throughout the day I decided to take a pregnancy test. Mickey had believed that he was not able to father children and had even explained to me before we got married that if I wanted children I may need to be aware that it wasn't possible. He called me from work the morning I decided I'd better take the test just to rule it out. At the time he was laying brick with his brother buddy. I casually mentioned I was ok but he may need to pick up a pregnancy test on his way home from work. He didn't wait for the work day to end he picked up the test and headed on home with it. He was anxious to know the results. I decided not to tell anyone yet because the tests are not 100% accurate. I went into our bathroom and took the test but I waited the few minutes for the results. While I was waiting for the results Mickey occupied himself with reading the back of the box the test came in. The box claimed the test was 99.9 % accurate. I was nervous to say the least. I sat there looking at the results for a few minutes. I couldn't believe my eyes! I was pregnant .I walked out of that small bathroom of ours and Mickey stood up and awaiting the results. I recall the exact words I said. I said, "If the test is right it looks like you are going to be a daddy". I held my breath and waited for his response. Mickey grabbed me picked me up and swung me around. He said, "So I am going to be a daddy?" He realized then that I was pregnant and he eased me down. I wasn't sure the floor was beneath me at this point. I was thinking yes you are going to be a daddy but I am going to be a mommy. I was scared. All kinds of thoughts ran through my mind. What kind of mother was I going to be? We "agreed" not to tell people until I went to the doctor and confirmed it. That night we went to a wedding and I heard Mickey announcing "it's 99.9% sure that I am going to be a daddy!" He just couldn't contain himself I had never saw a man so happy! With pregnancy came a lot of changes. I had all of the usual changes but with my pregnancy I became more clinging toward Mickey. He felt smothered sometimes. I wanted to be with him no matter where he was. God only knows how many pool halls and bars we went to while I carried our son. I didn't drink but I would get decaffeinated cokes or juice. I seemed to hunger for the nights I got to go and watch him play pool as much as he wanted to play pool. I was amazed by what he could do on that pool table. I had never seen anything like it! There were some times he'd "run the table" if he got a shot. He seemed to have a hustler's heart. He'd bet on the games he'd play and most of the time he'd win. In fact the games he'd lose I later found out he'd lose on purpose to get people to play with him. We didn't have an abundance of money. I recall a couple of times being broke. He'd write a check for a small amount and have the bar owner cash it for him. He'd play pool then he'd win the amount of check plus more. He'd usually get the original check back then by giving the man cash for it so he could tear it up before we left the bar. The hustler's life was new to me and sometimes it was exciting. There was a bad side to this type of lifestyle too. The rooms where he played were always smoke filled. The smoke irritated my eyes so I carried eye drops. The nights were always long. I would be sleepy and/or tired but Mickey was either winning or "down some money" so he'd want to stay. I refused to stay home and rest because I wanted to be with him. He'd try to get me to go home and rest but I would insist that I was all right. Pool playing was once again becoming his obsession and he was my obsession. He'd allow me to go with him because I was so desperate to spend time with him. Later he even taught me how to place bets on the side so we could make more money. One night a man took my chair when I had gone to the bathroom. Mickey kindly explained to the man that I had been sitting there and had gone to the bathroom. He went on to explain that I was his wife and I was pregnant. He asked the man if he didn't mind could he let me have my chair back. The man turned towards Mickey and used an ugly word in his response and he kept sitting in the chair. Mickey slapped him with an open hand and knocked him out cold. Mickey then turned to me as if that was nothing and calmly said, "There's your chair back, baby". I overheard someone yelling "get Moody" as another man dragged the unconscious man to the side to allow him to "come around". To that the man replied, "If you want Moody get him yourself!" The owner of the bar liked Mickey and so when the man did come around they asked him to leave. As crazy as it sounds Mickey continued the pool game that he'd been playing. Nothing seemed to shake him. We'd hear "last call" a lot of nights before we'd head home. We'd try to go places that they didn't know him so I could bet on the side. The more he played the more they got to know him. He always had told me that I could "surprise him" anytime he was playing. He tried to reassure me that he played for money and did not have any interest in another woman. As our baby grew inside me so did my insecurities. I found out where he was playing one night after I had told him I was staying home to rest and I decided to surprise him. I hated the way I felt and I knew I needed to learn to control my jealousy. I needed to be sure of him so I went to the bar. What I discovered only made me feel worse about my suspicions. He was so glad to see me that I felt like a pure fool! He explained he was just about to call me and try to get me to come on down because "fast Eddie" was there. I had no idea who fast Eddie was. I had not seen the movie they made about him called the color of money. I have since seen the movie. That night I had a tableside seat to watch the real Fast Eddie in action. Mickey even managed to get a poster of him that night and have him sign it for me. Often times, Mick would order food for me and have it delivered to me at the bar if it wasn't a bar that served food. He tried to make sure that I was eating right. He'd beg me to rest more because he'd feel bad about keeping me up so long. There were times when I had to work or that he'd insist I had to rest that I wouldn't go with him. He'd sometimes be gone for days and I wouldn't know where he was. He'd eventually call and I'd cry. He finally did get better about calling to "check in" and let me know he was okay. People thought that I was crazy to hang on to him but they didn't see the full picture. He always thought that he was taking care of me. He'd play pool until his hands were green from the felt on the tables. I watched it become "a job" to him. Some of the fun of watching him play was diminished when I saw him lose or when he'd played for days on end without rest. Anything would spur him on like realizing that we were out of potatoes at home. He told me how he wanted to give me the world and he couldn't even keep me from running out of potatoes. At the time I didn't realize how hard Mickey's life had truly been. He had done a lot of things just to survive from childhood to adulthood. Lack was something that he'd had to face growing up and so now he fought against it with everything in him. There were times the bar maids would call me to come and get him because he was exhausted, drunk, or both. There were "deals" that was made before we even got married. Plans had been put into action. The plans where things that I knew nothing about and he made sure that he "protected" me from for my own safety. There were things that were done right under my nose that I was naïve to. He became even more protective of me during my pregnancy in some regards. He wanted me to quit work and rely on him to take care of me but I wouldn't do it. I recall just a few weeks into my pregnancy jumping up too fast to silence the alarm before it woke him. I fell right onto my backside. He jumped out of bed faster than he ever had to pick me up and make sure that I was all right. He tried to get to me quickly if he thought I really needed him. The birth of our son Braxton Lee Moody was an amazing thing that we shared. There had been many nights since we were married that I was alone but he was there for me during the birth of our son and for that I was thankful. I will always thank him and God for that. The birth of a child is such a special time. We had an hour drive to get to the hospital (Dothan al, Houston co) I had been having contractions for weeks but then they'd stop. Mick jokingly told me, in the beginning of my pregnancy; that he could just deliver it at home with a little help from whisky. The closer the delivery time came though the more nervous he got. He started telling me he didn't want to deliver it at home after all and he feared I'd wait too late to get to the hospital. He actually would set up and feel of my stomach trying to time my contractions so he could get me there in time. He had talked to our son during the time I carried him. He woke me up more than once with a cold stethoscope on my stomach "talking to his boy". And he'd wake me when he felt him kick to make sure that I had felt it too. There was so much we got to share together during these times that now are good memories for me to recall. He drove through floodwaters to get me boiled peanuts that I wanted. He overpaid for the first watermelon of the season because I wanted it. He drove back to Alabama from Florida to get me a coke ice-e then drove back to Florida. I can honestly say I had no cravings during my pregnancy that he didn't make sure that I had. Finally we were told to be at the hospital the next morning bright and early so they could induce me. He drove half the way but then stopped to get a snack to settle his stomach and informed me we'd just be safer if I drove. That was strange because he hated to let me drive. I was getting a little concerned at this point I wondered just how much help he was going to be during labor. When we arrived at the hospital he did the paperwork while the nurse started the pit drip in the IV. My mom surprised me and was there too. Mickey asked the nurses to just keep me as comfortable as possible and they did. During the most intense part of the labor and delivery it was as if I had tunnel vision. I became unaware of anyone except Mickey helping me. Up into this point I knew my mom was helping comfort me and the nurses were talking to me. While I was in this" tunnel "it was as if I heard and saw only Mickey. He talked me through every contraction and every push. Seconds after Lee was born I looked around and saw everyone and was once again aware of their presence. The whole process itself was such a miracle! It was such a beautiful experience my heart will never forget the joy I felt. Mickey cut our new baby boys cord. After they had cleaned him up a little Mickey handed me our son. The joy that I felt was incomparable with anything I've ever experienced before or since. Mickey took pictures of me laughing and crying at the same time. The first words that I spoke over him were "he's a good boy!" Lee was born just as I had predicted when the sun went down. He was born September 27, 1994 at the precise time that the sunset that night. (Three minutes until 7 pm) Maybe that is why sunset is my favorite time of day. With the birth of every child comes the birth of new feelings. I felt overwhelmingly responsible to not only take care of Lee but to protect him from all of the bad that this world houses. I loved Mickey with all of my heart but I felt that Lee needed me more than Mickey did for a while. There had been times that I felt pushed aside by Mickey's lifestyle so I filled the emptiness I felt with our son. I didn't realize that Mickey had felt pushed aside himself as I reveled in my new role as momma. He loved Lee and was super protective of him. The roles of motherhood and fatherhood are as different as male and female. We humans are complex creations made in the image of God himself. I believe that it is only as we age do we truly learn who we are. In time, we learn to see our spouses as they really are too. In the beginning of a relationship we have such illusions of who our mate is. As we learn to see each other through realistic eyes we learn what real love is. Raising a child is such a great responsibility. From conception each child is given two parents for a reason. God knew that it would take the combined logic of a father and the nurturing of a mother to train up a child. In an ideal world all children would have two parents to raise them. Even when one parent is away they can still help the child in ways that only faith can understand, just by coming into agreement. Mickey has done a lot of time during Lee's life but he has always remained connected to him. He has been home with us for years at a time and in prison for years at a time. Through all of our struggles to keep our little family united God has been faithful. We all have had our difficulties but we talk honestly about our feelings. We have learned to love each other unconditionally. To love without condition is not a natural thing it must be learned .The reward of loving people like this is great. No love is without costs. We did not deserve the love that Jesus showed us. His love for us cost him his life. Love is so much more than a feeling. Real love requires action. I believe that God has a perfect plan for each of our lives and that he reveals it to us only in parts. If he had chosen to show me the things that Mickey and I would have to go through to reach our destiny I may have been fearful. I know that God's grace is sufficient to carry us through all things. Our minds know this but sometimes our hearts lose grasp of it. There is no way that I could share every experience that we have shared with you in this little book of mine. Mickey has experiences that I can only imagine. Talk about baggage the two of us had it! Somehow, we managed to see each other clearly through all of the mess that we carried. It was as if from the very beginning, we found in each other, a kindred spirit. Somehow it was as if he understood me. He seemed to see through the mask of pretense that I wore. No matter what I thought I never could fool Mickey. He seemed to always have the ability to see right through me. There were times when I thought he had chosen to look through me, as if he could no longer see me. Those were the bad times in my life. It is because of the grace of God that we are still together. Like I said earlier Mickey had experiences that I can't fully understand and those experiences affected us. I also had things that I hadn't dealt with. The next parts of my story are not always in order. There were times that my thoughts were just too jumbled to write. There were days that things were just too raw to share with anyone. For obvious reasons there will be some things that I chose not to share. It is my prayer however that some of the things we do chose to share will help someone to just have hope enough to hang on through what may be a hard place in their own life. Things are not always good nor are they always bad. When Lee was just a few months old, Federal marshals came to our home. They had come to "offer us a deal". Mickey had gotten himself into a mess again this time it was drug related. I felt like I had been dropped into a movie scene this couldn't really be my life. I was instructed to just sit still as they searched our house. I was draped with a blanket and tried to stay calm enough to continue feeding our son. Mickey told me to just sit still and do not answer any questions. He was as cool as a cucumber. The marshals talked to him about their "investigation". He knew they had been watching him because he had watched them too through a pair of binoculars. They were talking to him as if he was in the mafia and I was terrified. The deal they put on the table was that in exchange for his "help" they'd put us in witness protection. We'd have to leave our home with only the clothes on our back and our son. However, we'd have to go in the middle of the night all three of our names would be changed and we couldn't take any pictures and/or documents not even baby pictures. Neither of us would be allowed to call and/or see our family members again. I couldn't believe my ears! Mickey declined their offer and was served papers about when he'd have to go to his court date. They had enough evidence on him to take him that day they told him but they wanted him to think over their "generous offer". The main reason they explained for not taking him was it would "blow their cover" and they were watching others. He told me that they didn't care about helping us and they were not concerned with my life or that baby I was holding. He told me that he'd do the time. They shook his hand and told him if he changed his mind before the court day to call them and they left us their card. I had never been so scared and shocked in all of my life! Mickey went to court and was found guilty. He was sentenced to serve his time in Texarkana Federal prison. He was allowed to sign a bond good for one month to get things in order at home and then he had to turn himself in. Once again the delay was not to undo their investigations on other people. They knew that if Mickey started his sentence their cover would be exposed. The people higher up in the drug world knew Mickey's name. I believe they still were in hopes he'd help them. We had a month together before we'd drive the long trip to Texas. During this month both of us struggled to come to terms with this sentencing. Texas was a long way from our home. We made more home videos with each other and with Lee. We tried to enjoy the time we had left together but the sentencing seemed to always overshadow whatever we did. I tried to be strong but it was hard because I was watching my whole world crumble at my feet. I was scared and I was sad to say the least. Mickey tried to dull his feelings with more drugs. It was hard on him too knowing he'd be leaving a young baby and wife behind. He knew I promised I'd stick by him but deep in his heart he must have questioned if I would. I was from a small town and knew nothing about traveling. Heck I couldn't even read a map. Our hometown only had a couple of traffic lights. Mickey thought we needed to make the most of our time and get away together for a little while. He took me to a friend's house in another state. The plan was that his friends would go with us to Texarkana and take Lee and me back home. One night the reality of all of this really hit me hard. We were at the friend's house in their guest room. Mickey was asleep finally. The last week had been real hard on him and he had abused his body with enough drugs to kill him. I tried to be quite and I eased myself down by the bed into the floor. This was killing me emotionally I wanted to collapse onto the floor and cry until the pain of it left me. I was so thankful that Mickey was asleep though and I didn't want to wake him. So I just sat there crying as softly as I could. Silent tears streamed down my face. Mickey sensed I wasn't in bed..I heard him say "aw baby, come here" and he lifted me back onto the bed somehow and held me close to him. He just let me cry as he held me as tight as I could stand. Thinking back on that now I felt loved because he didn't try to fix it. He just let me feel what I felt. He was not always a man of a lot of words. There have been times when his actions said more than his words could have expressed. Before our trip began Mickey and his friend took a trip of their own. Each of them gave the other a shot of cocaine. I had never been around anything like that. I still recall the look of terror that rested in his friend's eyes as Mickey "talked him down" as he called it. He paced back and forth like a caged animal. He calmed down. It took him a little while to transform back into the man that I recognized as Mickey's friend from the one the drug created. Mick explained that he'd had "a bad trip". So many of my stories may refer to people as friends as to protect their identity. We managed to get to Texarkana somehow. Everything in us wanted to keep driving across the Mexican border but Mickey knew that a life on the run wouldn't be a life for us. We stopped at a rest stop and walked onto the grass together one last time. We had to get him on to prison by a certain time. I felt like we didn't have enough time together as it was and here we were limited again. I wanted him to know how much I loved him no matter what and that I'd wait for him. Finding the right words was not possible I felt like my heart was being ripped from my chest leaving me hollow. Without Mickey, that's how I felt. We had hugged each other a lot at the rest stop. It was a good thing that we had said our goodbyes because once we pulled onto the prison grounds he was told to remove all jewelry and go into prison immediately. No time was permitted for us there. We were not even allowed to walk in with him. We were instructed we were to leave grounds immediately after we dropped him off. I watched the man that I loved with my entire heart walk into those federal doors alone as we pulled from the property. I felt alone too but I wasn't really alone. I reached for our son, Lee. I removed him from his car seat and I held him next to me. Millions of worries and questions raced in and out of my mind. Our friends drove us home. How we got there I don't even recall. I just remember wondering how I was going to manage all of this. I was thankful that I had Lee it was as if I had part of Mickey with me all of the time. I didn't try to fight the depression to begin with it was as if it was a welcome friend. I slept as much as Lee did. I didn't want to open the curtains or see anyone except Lee. My brother came to see me and he sensed that I needed more help than I let on so he stayed with me a little while. He kept Lee some when I returned to work. Everything seemed to have become drudgery. I worked because I had to. I craved the still darkness of my room but Louie insisted I'd be ok. I was "strong", He said. He knew what I wanted was Mickey so he promised to take me as soon as I was permitted a visit. For the first time since he walked into the darkness of the prison I had a glimmer of light peaking through into my dark world. Up until this point Lee was my only sunshine. Yes! Just the chance to see Mickey lifted my spirits. My brother and his girlfriend borrowed a car and took me to Texarkana Federal Prison. This time we were directed to a speaker where we were asked if we had any weapons, drugs, etc, etc. with us. What kind of crazy questions where they asking? Where they insane themselves? Who pulls up to a federal prison and says, "Yes we have a carload of weapons and drugs? The rules and regulations were overwhelming. I was dog-tired. We had driven straight through Texas all night. We had stopped to clean up a little at the same rest stop that Mickey and I said our goodbyes at. I had worn a jumpsuit and it was sleeveless. I was told that I couldn't visit "without sleeves". Only Lee and I could visit since my brother and BJ wasn't on the approved visiting list. They didn't seem to mind. Louie even gave me his shirt to cover the jumpsuit. They said I could keep the shirt over it and visit. I was limited to 2 or 3 diapers for the day and a bottle or two. Lee's little diaper bag was searched for any "contraband". After filling out paperwork and going through metal detectors we still had to gain "clearance" to proceed. The others visiting had to go through the same procedures. We all were given instructions and verbally reprimanded if we did any of it wrong. The metal detectors were set off by shoes, bras, belts, jewelry and more things than a person in my state of mind could even had imagined. We had to have two kinds of identification on us. We had some type of ink that wasn't visible to the naked eye stamped onto our hands. We were told when to place our hands under a special light that made to ink on top of our hands visible. We were instructed not to wash the top of our hands or we may have difficulty leaving the prison. Leaving foot I thought will I ever get into here to see Mickey this was a terrible experience so far. We finally got "clearance" and were escorted by groups through heavy metal doors equipped with loud buzzing sounds. I heard the officer say stop at the yellow lines. There on the sidewalks were brightly painted wide yellow lines. If anyone crossed the yellow lines without being told to the officers scolded them. Waiting at a yellow line? Who would have known to do that? I had a lot to learn about all of these "rules". Officers that spoke to me on the first day seemed to speak down to me and I must have cowered beneath them. Our ID's were checked and double checked at several checkpoints before finally reaching an area that looked pretty much like a cafeteria of some sort. In this room would be where Mickey would join us after he got clearance for our visit. There were rolls of vending machines around the outer edges of the room. Mickey had told me I could bring in change in clear bag for machines. I had managed to bring the change money was tight right now for us. I had Lee and was accustomed to having Mickey help with expenses but for now it was all on my shoulders. I felt like the weight of the world rested on my shoulders. Mickey had told me a real kiss and hug was allowed when we first saw each other and when we said goodbye. I wondered how I could relax enough to kiss him with a room full of people there not to mention the watchful eye of the guards. I sat down where I was told to and waited. Lee was curiously looking around but he didn't really understand all of this yet. To say I was stressed would have been a gross understatement. It seemed like a long time passed before I finally caught a glimpse of Mickey walking across the prison yard toward us. I was emotionally distraught by the time he reached me just from the process I had to go through to get to him. He walked up to me and put his arms around me. I almost collapsed in his arms. Where he got the strength to hold me up I will never know. Here I was in Texarkana but I had no idea what roads we took to get there. The distance that lay between our home and here seemed to mock me. I had no idea how I could get back here and/or when I could. I felt overwhelmed and small. Mickey seemed to have all of the confidence in the world in me. He implied that this was nothing I couldn't handle. I had never felt so unsure of myself. I was wondering if I could go through all of this again. It was such a difficult ordeal just to get in. He suggested that I treat myself to a cappuccino from the machine to help me calm down a bit. Within the next hour I was much calmer and enjoying our visit. Lee went right to him and for a little while I actually felt better. It was good to see him and talk to him face to face. We had to limit our phone calls because they were costly but today my words were unlimited and I liked that! He tried to help with Lee as much as he could during our visit. Lee was so happy to see his daddy that I knew I'd have to get him back here somehow to see him. I fell asleep for a little while leaning on Mickey's shoulder and its sad to say but it was the best slept I'd had in months. I survived my first visit .Leaving Mickey after our visits was always hard. I cried almost every time that I had to leave him. He hated to see me cry. I would not look back as I left the prison so he couldn't see the tears that streamed down my face. My brother drove us back home and I tried to pay close attention to the roads he took. Once the visit was over and I was back home the heaviness searched me out again. I ached to be with my husband. It was as if I had to go through a period of grieving. I hated to leave the house because I was afraid he'd call and I'd miss the call. We survived the time apart with letters and phone calls. We learned to look ahead towards our visits. It gave us something to look forward to. Mickey gave me a phone number of a woman (Barbra) whose husband was an inmate too. She had a small daughter around our son's age. She had not been able to visit her husband because she had limited funds and no transportation. The thing is that she had been a truck driver in the past so she knew the ins and outs of traveling the interstates. I called her and we planned our first of many trips together. We hit it off right away. I learned a lot from her about traveling. I'd ask to work a long stretch so I could travel to Texas and back on my four off days. I tried to go every month. Barbra and I would make plans on when we'd be traveling together. Mickey was glad that I had someone to travel with me. She helped me with the driving. I was usually too tired to want to see any "sites". I'd want to get there as soon as possible and check into our motel. I was exhausted. She teased that I drove places like a man hardly stopping at all. I'd try to stop only to go to the bathroom and to refuel the gas. Sometimes we'd stop and eat. I preferred to get it to go plus we packed all kinds of snack foods and/or a cooler to save money. I watched every penny. I learned to be more independent than I was accustomed to being. After all Mickey wasn't there to "fix the sink" or do all of the tasks that husbands handle. Barbra commented a few times that I never wanted to see any sites. To me the whole trip was a "site". Remember, I was from a small town. I saw my first oil wells on the trip. I hadn't traveled a lot at the time. There were a couple of trips that we'd drive through the night and visit in the morning. We must have been a "site" ourselves! I knew that I looked rough to Mickey because I was so haggard from the trip not to mention working like I was. I'd try to save enough money to get a cheap motel. I wasn't too picky about the room as long as it was clean. Mickey had discouraged me from sleeping at the rest stops which we had done a time or two. He said he'd rather space out the visits if I couldn't afford a room. I tried to stay within a budget as much as I could. I even took on extra little part time jobs. One of my little jobs was babysitting kids at their house because it meant I could take Lee with me. I knew that he needed me and I tried to spend as much time with him as possible. My family helped me when they could. They'd help babysit Lee or buy diapers or things we needed if I was running a little short of money. I had thought about moving to Texarkana but Mickey said no. He thought I needed to stay closer to our families. There were times I could hardly afford a book of stamps. I'd restock stamps on payday so I could write Mickey. That was a treat for me just to have a whole book or maybe two of stamps. I tried to write him every day. I felt guilty if I missed a day. I knew that the inmates made it through a lot of rough days by hearing their names at mail call. Plus our phone calls were limited so I rarely got to tell him everything I wanted to before the phone call was cut off. Mickey was my best friend as well as my husband. I wanted to tell him about my day every day. I sure have had some experiences because of his doing time I can say that my life has never been boring! On one of our many trips we had a flat tire. My daddy had taught me how to change tires years before when I was first learning to drive. I wasn't incapable of everything. I had gotten out to change the tire but the lug wrench wouldn't break the thing loose. Barbra tried too. A man stopped to help us and told us the lug nut was stripped! He went on to say we'd need a power tool to break it loose. Then he left us there. I tried not to panic. Think Regina think .I spotted an exit across from us so I decided if Barbara would stay with the babies I'd just walk over and find a station. I thought I could find someone to help us there. Then I thought pray first. So I said a quick prayer something like Lord, please send me an angel. I said it out loud and I heard Barbra chuckle. Then no quicker than I said amen a truck stopped behind the truck was a trailer of some sort. I couldn't believe my eyes the man that swaggered toward us this time looked like a biker. He was dressed in the finest leather. He even sported a red bandanna. He looked like a giant standing there beside me as I explained we needed a power tool. He laughed and said what do you think I have in the trailer? It's full of power tools! He quickly produced the proper one and as I held the tire tool he changed our tire. He seemed to help us and be gone before we knew it. We got back into the security of our car and headed back onto the interstate. Barbra just sat looking at me and I finally said, "What is it?" She smiled and said how about the next time you pray being specific. I didn't know what she meant but she went on to say when you pray for an angel ask God not to send one that looks like a hell's angel please. I just laughed. I didn't care what he looked like but until this day I can't help but wonder if just maybe he'd been a real angel. I told her about a biker's bar Mickey took me to a couple of times. It seemed like everything jogged a memory of him for me. More than once when we traveled we'd have a problem and I'd pray out loud and God would answer me and help us. I saw a lot of things traveling and I saw a lot of things in the visiting at the prisons too. I sometimes saw things that I didn't understand or like. There was this time that we had gotten clearance into the visiting room and I witnessed something that really bothered me. I realize that inmates are there to be punished but this was the cruelest thing I had ever seen. The inmate's family had gotten clearance to see him and the guards explained to the wife that the visit would be short because he was being punished. She looked as tired as I felt. She waited for a long time with the kids. I watched, as they grew restless. Then when I thought she couldn't wait any longer they brought in the inmate. The kids all started chanted daddy there's my daddy. Then before they even let them hug him the guard turned him around and announced sorry your time is up the visit is over. The kids were left there with this woman screaming for their daddy. I recall a lot of cruel things being done that I thought were not necessary. Although I looked forward to our visits most of the trips drained me. I had problems sleeping without Mickey. I'd try to sleep just a few minutes on his shoulder sitting upright in the chair beside him when I visited. He'd hold Lee so that I could sleep a little. We had to limit amount of time when we did this because some of the guards frowned on it. I will admit some of them took pity on me and allowed me the luxury. Sometimes they'd tell him to wake me up and make me sit up though. It's sad to say but it was the best sleep I'd get for the month. I happened to be going to visit one day when they were bringing in new inmates. We were instructed to go back to our vehicles and wait until they told us they we could come in. I didn't know what was going on until the bus of inmates pulled up to the parking lot. There were several inmates inside of a bus. I could see that inside the bus was a cage like area. The inmates were shackled on their legs cuffed and all chained together. Gunmen escorted them into the prison and we had to wait until they were secured inside before we were allowed to get out of the car. I couldn't help but wonder who they were. They must have been really mean. I thought for them to have all of this security just to transport them. When we got into visiting area I proceeded to tell Mickey all about the way they brought in the new inmates. He laughed and told me that they were all brought in that way. During the visits they would occasionally blink the lights. I learned that the blinking lights was a signal for the inmates that if they needed to go to the bathroom that was the time to go. They were not allowed to go to the bathroom until they were told that they could. I didn't want to miss one minute of time with Mickey so I'd use the time myself to go to the visitor's bathroom. I'd also change lee if he needed it then. I felt like I could urinate on command too. I'd joke with Barbra that I sure hoped no one blinked their lights at me on the way home. Especially once we were on the interstate or it would force me to exit or pee in the seat. During Mickey's stay at Texarkana he tried to do little things for me. He thought that it would help me through the "down time" as he called it. He could no longer buy me things but he searched for things to "surprise" me with. Although it was against the rules he'd slip little treasures out to me. The first "gift" he brought out to me in the visiting area was a purple and yellow pansy that he had pressed in the clear wrapping from a cigarette pack. I laminated the whole thing once I got home and made a bookmark for my bible from it. He told me when he presented it to me that" although I deserved roses this was the best that he could do right now". Later he did manage to have me a dozen roses delivered to me at work with the help of a family member. I didn't know at the time how he had managed it but the fact that he did made me cry. He had even made sure that the roses were purchased from the same florist that he used to buy me flowers when he was at home. He amazed me the way he could pull off little things like that just for me. Another gift that he gave me was sharks teeth. I still have them too. I would like to have them made into a bracelet somehow. I thought of Jonah when I saw the sharks teeth, I felt like lately I could relate to him. It was as if we too, had been swallowed up by a whale, because of our disobedience to God. A gift that touched me too was tiny seashells. He found them in the prison yard in the same area he'd found the shark teeth (Coleman Florida). He gave them to me because he recalled me telling him about the seashells that my "Ma" had in my childhood. It meant a lot to me that he remembered how I told him they made me feel at peace. In his way he was trying to help me to have peace in the midst of this turmoil that we were in. It was rumored that the prison was once under water that is why they found shells and sharks teeth on the grounds. Lee never seemed to be afraid in the prison. Even as a child he accepted things as they were. He had struggled to walk at home. During one of our many visits he saw Mickey walk into the visiting room and he ran to him yelling "my daddy". Not every mom can put in the baby book beside of the words first steps taken in federal prison. Lee didn't mind getting his hand stamped before a visit either in fact he loved it! It came to be so "normal" to him that he'd hold out his little hand at the cashier's who took my checks. The ladies at the grocery store would have to stamp his hands after they stamped the back of my checks. They'd comment about how "he must have been to the fair". I wouldn't comment just smile and think, "yes, we are on quite a ride but it doesn't involve a Ferris wheel". During the time away from his son Mickey tried to do things for him too. He insisted that I sell his ladder and buy Lee a fish tank for his first birthday. I hated to sell any of his things but I knew it was important to him to contribute and to help with Lee. I already had to let his new truck be repossessed just so I could make ends meet. I felt bad and relief at the same time when they came and picked it up. On Lee's first birthday he got the fish tank that his daddy paid for and I had added several colorful fish myself. Lee loved to watch the fish and like his daddy he felt the need to help provide. He must have because he'd try to feed them anything and everything like whole pieces of bologna. He liked to walk up to the tank and bump it and make the fish move. He didn't remember doing this as a child and laughed when I was telling him about it years later. Uncle Milton overheard the story and Lee's laughter and thought it necessary to tell "another fish story". He told my son about how I used to "talk to his fish". He had an intercom behind his fish tank and he'd sneak out and talk to me from outside through the intercom. I was a little girl and so naïve that I believed his fish could talk! When he caught me watching the fish back out he'd go and talk to me through the speaker. I spent a lot of time talking to those fish and because I saw their mouths move and heard the voice I believed they talked to me too! I'd stand there in front of the tank in awe as I heard "what's your name little girl" and although I was timid I'd say "Regina". Then I'd brag to all the neighborhood kids "my hippie uncle has talking fish". I suppose they thought I was quite the storyteller. Lee found this story to be a hoot! He laughed and prodded Milton to "tell him more stories about things his mom did when she was little." He didn't have to prod too hard though before Uncle Milton told him about the parrot. I'd spend hours on end arguing with his ex-mother-in-laws bird. All it would say to me is hello Joe. I'd try to reason with the dang thing that my name wasn't Joe! Inmates are placed in levels of security depending on their scores. They are all scored depending on past arrests and/or crimes. Mickey would move down in level of security as time passed. When inmates are moved they are moved without notifying family members. Some of the time they don't even know that they are moving until they are told to pack up. Often this may be done in the middle of the night. I suppose this was for security reasons. What this meant to me was that if I sent him money he may not get it there and I'd have to resend more as soon as I could to the new place. Also there may be days before he was allowed to call me from the new address depending on their rules. So it meant I might go days without hearing from him. The first time this happened I was beside myself by the time he was allowed to call me but I soon learned the procedure and tried to settle into it. It wasn't always easy though not knowing if he was okay. I'd try to think like he used to say "no news is good news" but it was hard to do sometimes. Mickey's first move from Texarkana was to Oklahoma City. He was awakened in the middle of the night and told he was moving but as soon as he was allowed to call me he said "you think the way they brought inmates in to Texas was strange wait until you hear how we were brought here!" He went on to tell me how he was driven almost the whole trip secured with guards the whole time then taken into a helicopter. He was actually flown to the top of the building and taken down into prison from the rooftop. Barbra's husband was moved with Mickey at that time so we could still travel together. Looking back I see that God always allowed things to happen so that I could handle this. I had managed to purchase a Buick. It was an older car and the heater was broken but it got us about. We'd just bundle up to travel long distances in it when it was cold. I had learned firsthand how to "make due". I recall driving to Oklahoma in that old car we had the "babies" bundled up with layers of clothes to keep them warm. Still, I found myself touching them regularly to make sure that they were warm enough. With all of the concern over them we somehow failed to bundle up enough ourselves. My feet have never been so cold! We'd have to stop more than we usually did just to warm up. It was freezing that night and my feet were so cold that they ached. How I wished we'd thought to layer socks on ourselves but at least the babies were cozy. Often time's moms think of the babies instead of themselves. Upon arrival to the prison grounds in Oklahoma we drove up to a big gate. Our identifications were verified and we were given permission to "proceed". I sat there for a few minutes puzzled by just how I was going to "proceed". In front of the car I saw huge steel beams all the way across the road ahead of me. The guard didn't attempt to explain. He disappeared back into the guard "shack" but within a few minutes I saw the beams lowering into the ground. Talk about security this place had it! Once they were lowered I drove across them. As I drove past them, I glanced into my rearview mirror. I caught a glimpse of the beams returning to rise up again. I was secured into the parking lot and prevented by leaving without authorization to do so from the powers that be. Basically the rules proved to be pretty much like the ones in Texas. Barbra and I were both tired but we were happy to see our husbands. Her husband started to share about a fellow inmate's recent "suicide" but Mickey hushed him. He went on to tell him that I worried enough already. When he was home later I learned that the "suicide" was in fact a murder by an officer. It made national news. Mickey's response was simply "that's why I wouldn't let him talk about it back then to you". Even then he was just so matter of fact about it. I know that there have been many times that Mickey chose to carry things quietly within his heart and mind. Of all of the things that I have learned from this side of prison life the truth is that he carries the brunt of it himself. Sometimes it's in quietness though that strength is revealed. My Uncle Milton helped me drive on one of the trips to Oklahoma when my friend couldn't go. We saw a small amount of snow but it was dirty and already melting. On the ride back home we ran into "frozen fog". We had never heard of it. Visibility was poor and we had to travel by using taillights from the big trucks. The fog thickened though so much that even the big trucks had to pull over. We followed suit and pulled over with the others to wait for the fog to lift. We spent a large part of the night by the roadside, just waiting. Finally the visibility improved and we all headed back onto the interstate. We were late getting home by several hours. Mickey had called our home so much our answering machine would no longer hold messages. He'd been terrified that something had happened to us. As we stepped into the door I answered the ringing phone. Mickey's voice trembled in response to my own. Was he crying? I heard him say "Thank God! He started praising God that we were home safely. I told him about the fog it turned out he'd never heard of it either. Together we have survived "time and time again". He served inside as we did time outside. Surviving prison time is hard on families as well as inmates. I myself have had many sleepless nights with concern about him. He has had the same being concerned about his family. One thing is for sure; it is not easy on either side of those walls. Sometimes I see the same quite strength resting within our son that Mickey possesses. I know that our strength truly comes from the Lord. Lee amazes me the way he handles things sometimes. He has even tried to help other kids whose dads are in prison. I am so thankful that this has not made him bitter but instead he has learned to take things as they come. Soon Mickey was moved again. This time he was taken to Coleman Florida. Rules remain similar between prisons but each prison seemed to possess its own personality. No vivid colors were used for the most part all of them had dull gray décor. Rules were usually strict. Proper procedure was to be followed by both the inmate and their families. It didn't take you long to learn the rules because if you broke them visits could be withheld. At the prison in Coleman we were not allowed to park on premises until it was time to visit. We were allowed to line up on the roadside just before entering the prison grounds. The lines were long. If you wanted to secure a place to get into visit early and before count time you had to line up extra early. The lines started forming before daylight and even then people would try to "race" to get ahead of you in line so you had to exit your vehicle swiftly when you could get onto grounds. Sometimes not being rude would jeopardize my place in line but as long as I wasn't too far back in the line I tried to be content. One of the most memorable things they done to me was giving me a visiting form in Spanish to complete. When I brought it to the officer's attention I was told, "Sorry that's all we have we are out of English." I just did the best that I could and filled it out. I still can't read Spanish unless you count the word taco. I had filled out these forms before so I simply guessed. I had no choice if I wanted to visit. Sometimes traveling to/from the visits was a hardship because of the distances. Everything had to be budgeted in from the motels to the vending machine money. Anything could happen while traveling. Adapt became a word that we had to become familiar with. With every move came changes some for the better and some for the worst. In Coleman we learned about a motel that catered to inmates families. The motel was called the Red Carpet Inn. It wasn't the Hilton but it was clean. Of course they profited from having the prison close but they gave us rooms for a discounted price. All we had to do is tell them that we were a "member of the Phoenix Club" which was the code for inmate's family. This allowed us to keep a bit of dignity when we checked in and other guests were around. The others must have wondered just what kind of elite club this was since we got discounted rooms. I was thankful not to have to explain our situation all of the time. I found the owners of the motel to be helpful and respectful. They always asked us if everything was okay and even made sure to give us extra towels. More than the towels they gave us something that prison life sometimes stripped from us, our dignity. Inmates have to be strip-searched and that in itself causes dignity to be misplaced within the system. The reason for such invasive searches is "to keep things from being smuggled in". The strange thing is that "contraband" still finds its way into the prisons. Inmates still can gain most types of drugs that they may want if they can afford them. Shanks (homemade knives) are still found regularly during a "shakedown". And many a bottle of julep and/or moonshine has been made within the prisons themselves. Safe is certainly not a word that comes to mind when I think about the inmate's environment. They become calloused to some of what they see. Often I'd react to some newfound knowledge about an incident that occurred and Mickey would act as if it were nothing. Often he'd remind me that he wasn't "in the boy scouts" but in prison. The prison life is not the easy road that society claims it to be. Survival is the main goal. The inmates learn to hustle money and/or things that they need. They learn to barter with what they have to obtain what they need. Things are sometimes bought and sold for profit. Coffee, cigarettes, stamps, or just about anything could be used as a tool to survive. Money can be sent to inmates by their families. Often times the money is limited because the family has to learn the skill of survival themselves. Most inmates learn to live on limited funds. Through the years I have saw some wealthy people incarcerated too. It seemed like they had it easier but in reality they still faced the same dangers that raged within the walls. Money doesn't always buy safety. The seasoned inmates seem to function beneath a code. The secrets of this code are not understood by the outside world. There are things that they don't tolerate between one another. They sometimes become intolerant to people on the outside as well. Maybe it's because they are forced to comply with so many rules that they vow to not live like that again once they survive it. They are expected to fit back into society immediately upon their release. Society has no idea what demons that have had to face and often times they are misunderstood. Inmates have saw such evils that we families can only imagine. If our environment shapes us into what we become then how are prisons supposed to "reform" anyone? God is the only way for restoration to occur. Our Father gives us the strength to not only survive this life but to live it to its fullest regardless of our valleys. We all face hard times in this life. No one is immune to them. True, we all face different kinds of problems but we all must face them. What we cannot face we can never conquer. Facing our problems head on is not always an easy task. Sometimes just facing ourselves is a serious undertaking.

Most often we bring on so many of our problems on ourselves. My grandma used to say, "You made your bed now lie in it". This was a saying that always puzzled me because she wouldn't even let us sit on a made bed let alone lie in it! People who have never had family members in prison sometimes think like that. Often I wonder if they would change the way that they view inmates if it was their loved ones within the system. I know firsthand that it would change. Not only would they change but also it would be a quick metamorphosis! What we see on the news and the media about how prisoners are taken care of by the government and the reality of it is sometimes two different things. People who have not walked through this place have no idea what it's like. One reason I wrote my little story is so that people who are in this place can know that they are not alone. There are people who have done this too. Someone out there understands just what you are going through and how badly you are hurting. God himself understands you. He will place people in your lives to help you but you have got to allow them to do so. Sometimes we want to isolate ourselves because we think no one would understand. We have to make room for others in our lives sometimes when we feel the most alone. That is hard for me to do but I am learning. In my past I always prided myself on my ability to "pull myself up by my own bootstraps". I have learned that we all need each other from time to time and there is no shame in admitting it. A closed heart is the worst type of prison. God in his wisdom moved my friend's husband to Coleman right along with Mickey. For a while I still had a traveling partner. Not long after Mickey arrived in Coleman he learned about the Phoenix club that I wrote about earlier. He was glad to pass the knowledge on to me. He knew that with our tight budget every little bit I could save helped. The catalytic converter on the red Buick had caught on fire and I was afraid to drive it. Not to mention the trunk got damaged. I had to put the spare tire in the back floorboard. This made us even more close traveling like that with two women and two babies, crowded was a better word. I felt like I had to pack so much already because of the little ones. I managed to get another car. I don't even recall the type it was all I recall was it was black and had four doors. The reason that I can't recall the model was probably because it lasted a total of one trip. It was used and when I say used I mean, no warranty. The old man that sold it to me saw me coming. It was clean was the best thing that I could say about the car. After one visit on it to see our husbands it stalled on me. I somehow managed to get it pulled off of the road and I called for help. I learned when my "help" came that the body of it had rusted into and shifted and was "totaled" possibly from an old wreck. It's a miracle they said that you got it off of the road and that you made it this far on the thing! We had to have it towed. Here we were two women with small children stranded hundreds of miles from our homes. I tried to stay calm and cool. I decided to go to nearby café and feed the children. That gave me a little time to "collect" myself. I ordered myself a coffee and forced myself to "relax". I thought about a possible solution. Everything in me fought the desire to panic. I wanted to cry but that wouldn't get us home. I choked back the tears and got out my address book. I thumbed through it and realized my Uncle Clayton was closer to me than anyone else right now by location. I knew that he could get to us quicker than anyone else in that address book. No one had cell phones back then so I took another swig of coffee and went out to the pay phone. Barbra watched the children while I went to make the call. I did not like to ask anyone for help but here I was in a situation again where I was forced to. I dialed the number and swallowed hard wondering if that was the last bit of my pride that I had just swallowed. He answered quickly and was on the way to get us. I don't recall how long we had to wait but I was relieved to see him pull up. We placed our belongings in his vehicle and he took us to his house for the night. He lectured us on the dangers we faced traveling to see "those husbands of ours" and we listened respectfully. There was not a single thing that he said that I hadn't thought about. We had to call someone to come and pick us up from Callahan Florida now. Like all girls do I called my daddy. He and my daddy in law agreed to drive on down that night and pick us up the next day. I tried to get the knot in my stomach to go away as I thought of those two traveling the interstates to get us. I walked through the pasture at Uncle Claytons trying to convince myself that they'd be okay. As I walked I thought about a happier time. My mind drifted back to a time when I was at his home before. I was a girl of twelve when I was last here. I was allowed to visit for a summer. I really had enjoyed that summer with my cousins (Penny and Beth). One of the best things about that summer so long ago was "Sugar" their pony. I got to ride her every day. I had always wanted a horse of my own and I loved my time with the pony. She was a gentle thing and the two of us became inseparable for those weeks. I'd gladly help with the chores no matter what the job. I knew that after the weeds were pulled or the house was cleaned that I'd get to ride Sugar. I had not had much experience riding before this summer. I had ridden before but I always had someone else in control then but now it was just the pony and me. I loved it! I was shown once how to saddle her and how to get the bridle and bit on. I was pretty much allowed to ride her whenever I wanted to. I liked to ride her without the saddle. I had trouble getting it tight .I remember throwing a blanket across her and trying to race across the pasture. I seemed to learn best hands on. It didn't take me long to realize the blanket would slide off and when it did so did I! Sugar was a good pony and she'd return to get me when I fell off. She'd stand there near me and wait for me to remount. Once she got too close and actually stood on top of my foot. It took me a few minutes to get her to move off of it. I wore that mark from the hoof print for the weeks to follow but I didn't care. As long as I could ride again all was right in my world. I got into the habit of making coffee and getting a snack ready for Uncle Clayton. When he came home he'd find it waiting for him. Sugar and I would find our way to his truck every afternoon because we knew he'd have something on there for her. I still have great memories of those first rides. A feeling of freedom came over me when I rode. Everything that bothered me seemed to be carried away by the wind that caressed my face as I rode. I still love to ride horses. A flood of memories of my childhood overtook me as I walked. I did get to sleep that night. I prayed that my daddy and daddy in law would be there safely. They appeared the next day as faithful as the sunshine and best of all no lecture awaited us. I could count on those two having my back even in the worse of troubles. I drove all of us home. I managed to get another car but it was a better one. Of course it cost me more than five hundred dollars but I was able to get payments low enough I could afford them. I didn't like having the payments but I knew I needed a safer car and I was relieved to have one. We made several trips back to Coleman. I tried to visit as often as I could. We'd go every month or at least every two months whenever money allowed it. I knew it was important that we visit if Lee and Mickey were to stay bonded as father and son. Children have a way of growing up much too fast. Time is a precious thing. That is why "doing time" is so hard. Thanks to the Phoenix club we were able to take a little "vacation" in Coleman near Mickey. We'd visit with him during the day and grill out by the pool in the evenings. I had learned to enjoy simple things like the pool and my son's laughter. We had taken along a portable grill so we didn't have to eat out as much. I don't know why we were referred to as the Phoenix club but it made me think about the myth of the Phoenix. In Greek mythology the Phoenix or the firebird lived five hundred to a thousand years then it would build a nest of myrrh. The nest and the bird would burn fiercely and be reduced to ashes. Some legends were that the bird would fly into the flames within the nest. A young Phoenix would then arise reborn from its ashes. The name of the club had significance to me even though I don't get into mythology. There have been times when I felt like we were almost destroyed then somehow God raised us up to enjoy life again. God never promised us that we wouldn't have difficulties in this life but he did promise he'd never leave us. We may go through the fire in order to become all that he has planned for us to become and yet we will not be destroyed by the fire. My faith hasn't always been strong. There have been times that it soared and times when it was difficult to muster up. Once when we were traveling home from Coleman our gas hand was low. I had twelve dollars and two drink caps where I had "won" two free drinks. I just knew God would provide. I put the whole twelve dollars in the tank and got the drinks for the children. I knew it was going to be close getting myself home plus Barbra .The plan had been to get to my house and Barbra's parents were to pick her up. The closer we got to Alabama the closer the hand went toward empty. I did the only thing I could. I prayed. I knew that God was faithful. The thing is that I had prayed out loud again which freaked out my traveling buddy. Every time the hand plunged toward the empty symbol I'd pray again. She was fretful and she'd bring my attention to it several times before we got across the Alabama line. I tried to reassure her that all was well. Every time I prayed the gas hand would move further from the "E". I joked and told her the "E" was for enough. She couldn't believe it but she swore the hand moved a little every time I prayed. I would have loved it to jump over to the full but it never did that. I just praised God for providing for me. We went by my daddy's house before going to my home. It was as if God had told my dad about our problem because just as I pulled into his yard he handed me enough money to fill up my tank. I didn't have to ask him for help. There were days like that where God made his presence known to me. Then there have been the days when to be honest I wondered where God was in my life. I am being honest here so that you know you are not alone if you think that way yourself. There will be days that are just hard. It will feel like the weight of the world rests on your shoulders and you will almost buckle beneath the load. Then there will be days when finally you feel the load has been lifted. Wait for those days. Do not give up. We shouldn't believe the lies that the devil tells but instead focus on God and who he says he is to us. God is the finisher of our faith. He began the work in us and he is capable of completing it. Not too long ago I was using a push mower to cut our grass out by the roadside. I noticed a dip in the yard where the grass grew taller. It was as if I heard God tell me it's in the valleys when we think we aren't doing so well that we grow the most. We have to develop the skill our hearing God for ourselves. If you ask him to talk to you and you listen for him he will teach you to hear him. He speaks to me in different ways. Sometimes he is silent. Learn to surround yourself with friends that encourage you. In time my traveling buddy's husband and my husband were sent to different places. By the time this happened I was confident enough to travel with just me and my son. I'd meet new people and sometimes we'd travel with others to help them or just to cut down on the cost. I was no longer terrified of the prisons. I had learned that if I could just get the hang of the rules at the new places that I could adapt. Most of us can adapt to just about anything when it is important to the well being of our family. Lee was so young that some of the things we did were like a game to him. When Mickey moved to Talladega we traveled a couple of times with people that we had known from our past. This family had a son that was overactive. He'd tell his mom he had to go to the bathroom but he'd wait until it was too late. In her wisdom she had solved the dilemma by keeping a cup with a lid on it in her van all of the time. Much to our surprise, when he announced he had to urinate; his mom handed him a large cup. After he used the cup she simply put the lid on it until she could empty it later down the road.

Lee wasn't about to be outdone so he wanted a cup too. Remember they were little boys at the time. It was no surprise to me when he ran and told his daddy "guess what I got to do? Mickey asked me when I approached him "why did Lee pee in a cup and put a lid on it?" I explained the whole situation and a smile came across his lips when I told him your boy wasn't about to be outdone. In Talladega they had a playroom for the kids. This was something new to us for the most part up until now kids had to sit with parents all day. It was as tiresome for them as for their parents so I was relieved for something to entertain Lee. There were times when Lee struggled with the fact that his daddy wasn't home but we never lied to him about it. As a young boy he assumed the role of protecting and looking out for me. I look at him today and I am amazed at how God has used him to help me through the years. As time passed Mickey was moved to a halfway house in Montgomery Alabama. I was even allowed to pick him up and drive him there myself. We got lost and I thought we were going to be late getting there so I was nervous. I didn't want us to start off at a new place on the wrong foot. Much to my surprise the people that ran it were nice to us when we arrived. They went over the basic rules with us and the other ones with Mickey later. This place was lower in security and we were actually allowed to have family outings. We could have picnics on the grounds or leave to get a bite together. After a set amount of time Mickey would get a job and be allowed to drive home on the weekends. He had a certain amount of driving time allotted to him. He was allowed passes for church but there again we had to be back at our home within a set time. The authorities at the halfway house expected him to call when he arrived and they'd call throughout the weekend even during the middle of the night to make sure he was there. Sometimes being called in the middle of the night was a hassle but I was thankful that he got to be home. On one of his trips home Mickey managed to stop long enough to buy me an anniversary present. Talk about surprised, I was. It was the cutest thing a little hummingbird whatnot. I liked it so much that Mickey soon started buying me all kinds of hummingbirds. In the years that followed he'd buy me a whole collection of them. He'd search high and low and come home with yet another one for "my collection". He was able to help a little more with Lee and I was glad to let him. Lee wasn't used to Mickey getting to go places with us he was accustomed to waving bye to him at the prisons. We fretted about how Lee would adjust but it was pointless because like always he adapted without any problem. On one of our outings Mickey took us to see a buffalo farm and Lee loved it! It didn't really seem to matter what we did as long as we were together. We finally made it through all of the adjustments and Mickey got to come home. There was still so much to overcome. There were problems that I didn't understand but I tried really hard to help. Mickey had problems getting and keeping a job back then. He didn't like to be told what to do in a condescending way. It didn't seem to take much to set him off. He was pretty tired of being told what to do and when to do it. He managed to get a job at a shipping plant for a while. He worked in the freezer. The job was on third shift and he didn't like that. He would have us come and eat with him sometimes in the middle of his shift because he missed us. He'd have Lee some chocolate milk set in there just long enough to be good and cold. He even had a man bring me roses that he'd grown. After he bragged to Mickey that he had some that looked like velvet. He hid them in the cooler until me and Lee arrived and surprised me with them. The roses were the deepest red that I had ever seen. They looked almost black and they did feel just like velvet! Mickey had his moments. He used to sing to me "once in a blue moon I do something right". I guess he really did feel like he rarely got things right because he couldn't see himself through my eyes. It seemed like he was always trying to do little things to show his love for us. As things would go he'd quit this job and work for himself for a little while. He had difficulties making decisions or staying focused sometimes. Trouble was once again seeking him. He had the best of intentions and yet it seemed like his plans just wouldn't come together. He returned to what I call an outlaws way of life. He found himself drinking and dabbling with drugs again. In the drug world you run into things and people that you just don't talk about. There is a vow of silence in this world so for obvious reasons a lot of details will be left out about this. Like Mickey I found myself in some dangerous situations although at this time I had never tried drugs. Mickey was asked to come over to a man's house to "talk". I knew the man was a small time dealer and since someone was watching Lee I insisted on going with him. I was asked to wait in the living room with the man's wife while he and Mickey "chatted". This wasn't strange to me because there was a lot I was sheltered from. I thank God for protecting us both in our ignorance. The man had guns pointed at Mickey in the other room and had told him that "they'd carry him out" Mickey had nerves of steel he actually walked out of the room right past the man and told me to "let's go". I was told the details of this later. This man had once called Mickey his friend .It would take him a long time to forgive the man. Thank God that now he can pray for the man. In the world that Mickey lived in women and children were left at home when "business was to be handled". I wasn't expected to ask questions about any of the men's business. There were times that I would try to but most attempts to ask questions was seen as trying to control him. The places that were deemed as "safe" were places that the women of this world could hang out together while the men "went out and about". It was as if people in this world had a mafia mindset. The kids played well together and we women would talk. We rarely talked about the reality of our situations. It was as if we were drawn into a fantasy world in which everything was "fine". Often times I'd fall asleep on our friend's leather couch awaiting the men's return. If I complained or confessed worry I thought the other women would have seen me as weak. The truth is that they were more like me than I realized .I had learned the art of pretending. Being married to Mickey I got to see things that most people only see at the movies. I have saw a close friend of his with a sawed off shotgun pointed out the backdoor of a shop pointed at the men that where talking to Mickey. He told me to "just sit down don't worry I've got his back". I had saw scenes like this in westerns as a child. It was strange to me that the men keep trying to reassure me "not to worry". As things would progress Mickey would have yet another run in with the law. He would drive right through a gate when the officers were firing at him. They later tried to convince him that it was night hunters he heard but he knew better. It took six or seven officers to book him that night. They sprayed him with maze and then hosed him down with water until he almost lost his breath. All of the excitement caused him to have chest pain so they took him to the emergency room. A nurse from the hospital called me and told me "he was in pretty bad shape" but felt that they couldn't give me further details. It was the middle of the night and I was scared he was real bad. I managed to get Lee dressed calmly. I grabbed the first thing I could find for myself and dressed not a thing I had on matched but I didn't care. I had to get to Mickey was all that I could think. When I walked into the emergency room an officer bragged to me that he "helped to bring him in". Looking at Mickey like this his remark angered me. I replied "well if I were you I wouldn't tell anybody after all it took six or seven supposedly young virile men to bring in one ole man". Mickey's heart enzymes were elevated which meant he was on the verge of a heart attack. They placed a guard outside of his door .I had to go sign a bond before the guard was permitted to leave. We had concert tickets for that night. Mickey was upset that he was "causing me to miss the concert". I reassured him that it was ok. It took both me, and the doctor to convince him to stay at the hospital. The doctor was kind to him and tried to explain his condition. He wanted to put him in the unit but Mickey refused. He wanted to smoke so the doctor told him he'd allow him to smoke there in the room just blow the smoke out the window. That was strange. He bent a lot of rules to try and keep Mickey there that night. I thought we'd convinced him to stay so I went out to the car. When I returned there he was up putting his blue jeans on. He had taken his IV out too. The doctor came back and tried to explain the danger of him leaving with his enzymes that high. He told him he could have a heart attack. Mickey told him that if he was going to have one no doctor could stop it. He just kept insisting that he was taking me to that concert. He told the doctor "Look doc she don't ask for much but my wife deserves a night out". He decided he'd take his chances and even joked with me that if he was going to have a heart attack he could think of another way to do it than sit in that hospital. I begged him to skip the concert. In the crowd I knew I wouldn't be able to get him help if he needed it. Mickey felt guilty for "all he was putting me through" but still the drugs wouldn't release their hold on him. He did end up going to jail but I wouldn't tell you where because of the crookedness of that place. This place was a joke! While he was there an officer would set up times where he could come to his office and visit with Lee and me. I could even bring him food during the visits. That in itself was okay I suppose but he'd later bring him to our home for some time as husband and wife. He'd wait in the living room for our time to be up. He told me that if he kept the inmates happy it made his job easier. That doesn't say much about the security of the place huh? We also were allowed to pick him up and take him to an optometrist to be fitted for glasses. Over the years I have saw things that were not "on the up and up" done by people in authority over the prisoners. While here Mickey would actually hand me out money with paperwork or old letters to help me with Lee. He could hustle money up and give it to me so I could take Lee bowling or something. The thing is the officers would hand it right over to me! Some of the workers were fired for taking things from the inmates funds themselves. I have met some good officers over the years but I don't assume that because someone is in authority that some don't misuse it either. This jail was just a place of "holding" and he'd leave it soon and go on down the road. Mickey went to a higher level of security but once again worked his way back down the system. At some point he went to a camp. I was able to take food to the camp in a cooler. He liked that because I could cook his favorite things and we cook picnic outside as a family. I had to provide Lee's birth certificate to prove he was his son and thus eligible to visit here. I didn't mind that because here they got to play. They'd toss around a baseball some but Lee's thing was football. I have a good snapshot of us with Lee holding his football a day that they threw it about. The visits were a little more laid back once you got clearance into the camp. Mickey found ways to surprise us with little gifts again here. I still have the sample bottle that he brought perfume to me in. He eventually got work release. At the work release job we were able to "run into each other" occasionally. Of course I'd have to drive for hours for this chance meeting but I was still in love with him so the miles were nothing. We'd look for any opportunity to steal some time together. Mickey's dad (Grady) would even go with us to visit at the camp sometimes but he was getting frailer. Grady held a big place in Lee's life and mine. He was a character! He added so much to our lives. Mr. Grady served in World War II as well as the Korean War. He was a staff sergeant (E6). He received the following metals for his service: European Middle Eastern Campaign, Silver Star, Fidelity Efficiency Honor, Army of Occupation Germany American Campaign and the World War II metal (The Bronze Star). There were many things in his life that he tried to keep hidden, as he did not want to appear weak in any way. He confided in me as we grew closer about a few of his regrets and hurts. He had made his share of mistakes as we all do. He and Mickey's mother went their separate ways years before. For all appearances he had moved on with his life. He even had a girl friend right up until her death. In the end it was "Bithee" as he called her that he grieved the most for. He shared things that had happened between them with me because he didn't want to carry it to his grave. It seemed that both of them had caused each other some pain but then I only heard his side of things. I never knew Mickey's mother (Tabitha). I have been told stories about her from others and she must have been a woman of great strength. In my heart I believe that she loved Grady until the day she died even though he had caused her pain. Usually it's only people that we love that can truly hurt us. Real love knows no end. Grady had softened somewhat in age by the time I met him. I did say somewhat because it seemed as though sometimes he was a tough old man. He had done a little prison time for murder (self defense) when Mickey was a young boy. This affected his children in ways that only they can tell you. He loved to gamble more than anyone I know. He'd tell me stories about how Tabitha would go and find him in the middle of a poker game and demand that he come home. He confessed that he wasn't a good husband to her. Then he'd smile a little and say but "I'd do things on purpose just to make her mad because I loved to get a rise out of her!" He didn't care what kind of gambling it was. He loved it all! He bet on football games, baseball, lottery, cards, or anything that presented itself. More than once I overheard him talking to his "bookie". He loved to look at Christmas lights. It became something that we'd do with him every year. On his last Christmas he'd mentioned wanting his own lights in the tree in front of his yard. I had no way of knowing that it would be his last Christmas but I felt an urgency to get those lights up. I recall how he fussed with me about climbing that ole tree to put them up. He told me "I'll have someone else do that Gal I don't want you to fall."   I ignored him and proceeded on. I could be just as stubborn as he was at times. He enjoyed those simple lights of his and I have always been glad that I put them up. He told me "I'd leave them up until August if people wouldn't make fun of me". He was always good to Lee and me. He was protective of us both. He said he was a better Papa than he ever was a daddy. He hated it if I had to spank Lee and he'd tell me "to take him home if you have to do that". He always managed to keep those little chocolate milk jugs in his refrigerator for Lee or "little Red" as he liked to call him. I tried to explain that it would be cheaper if he bought the bigger ones but he had a rebuttal ready for that. He informed me that the little ones with the handle was more Lee's size and he could hook his little hand around the handle. So my point was moot. He was a peculiar man when it came to shopping. He used to have me go to two grocery stores because one had milk with a certain color lid and the other had tea with another color lid. He thought that neither one of them would be as good for some reason if it didn't have the same color of lid that he was used to buying. I know it was crazy but I obliged him and made sure we got it actually where he wanted. His daughter Jeanette was coming to take him to the drugstore one afternoon he told me but then he called frantic because she hadn't made it. I had been working in my rose beds and looked a mess but I sensed the urgency in his voice. He told me the store would close soon. I reassured him we'd be right there. I washed my hands. Lee and I made it to his house in record time. He was waiting in the yard pacing when we arrived. Thank God we made it before the store closed so he could get his medicine! Much to our surprise it wasn't medicine he was after. He wanted to buy a mop! He'd saw the brand advertised on TV as a better mop than the brand he'd been using and he wanted it right then. It's no wonder Jeanette didn't race right over I thought, now that I knew the whole story. He loved his little garden and he kept one as long as he could. He always wanted me to go with him "to help him pick out his tomato plants". The thing is he knew actually what kind he wanted but he'd never admit he just wanted to hang out with us. He brought us a big basket of peaches and told me that he was going to charge me the peelings for the peaches. I thought that he was just joking but I found out that he really wanted me to peel them and return the peelings so that he could make jelly. Of course when I returned them I hung around to watch him make the jelly because I never had heard of doing it from peelings. He loved to go out to eat and his favorite places were buffets. He enjoyed his car and he wanted it to look "sharp". When he wanted us to take his car anywhere he always wanted his country tapes playing. There was a small country service station in the town he lived that he frequently visited. The men there treated him like extended family. They expected to see "Mr. Grady" daily. If they didn't see him they'd give me a call and ask me to go and check on him. He liked to go by their station every day and get a pack of cheese crackers from a certain shelf and a coke. He'd just sit around at the counter on a stool and visit while he had his snack sometimes he'd answer the phone for them if they were pumping gas. His driving got worse as he aged and if I was not there to drive him he'd ride his electric scooter to the store. He'd drive it about anywhere too if we didn't watch him. He told me once he'd planned to drive it down to the Florida line and buy lottery tickets. I convinced him to wait until I got off from work and I'd take him myself. There was a lady in her forties that worked there. Grady was in his eighties. He'd buy her a coke when we got ours and his tickets .She told him once she wished she could go with us when he shared our plans to go see Christmas lights that night. She was just being friendly but Grady mistook it for interest in him. He wanted to go back the next day and buy her another coke. I humored him and drove him back. When we left the store that day, he said "She's older than I thought!" He lost interest in her because of "her" age I thought and I held back a chuckle. Lee has fond memories of their exchange of "see you later alligator" and "after while crocodile" as well as several great memories of him. Mickey was scheduled for release from the camp but the exact date of release was pending. Grady was growing weaker and he told me that he would give me gas money if that was the hold on him coming home. I explained that I had gas money it was the government we were waiting on telling me when I could get him. I worried a bit when he told me that "he needed Mickey" because all of the years that I had been married to Mickey he never "needed" him. He depended on me to take care of most of his things not Mickey. He refused to let Mickey write out a check for him years before and told him he'd "just wait for Janice to do it". I knew in my heart that something real bad was wrong if he wanted to see Mickey. I asked him why he needed him he just hem-hauled about and told me "I just need him". I knew that both of them had things unsaid between them. Before Mickey's release Grady was hospitalized and I promised him I'd get Mickey to him. I drove up to the camp not sure if the paperwork would be there that morning or not we were told it was supposed to be in the mail. I knew that Grady's time was short and I felt pressed to get his son to him. When I arrived I was told no mail had arrived yet but I could wait for it. If paperwork was there Mickey would be free to go if not he'd have to wait for paperwork. After what seemed to be a long wait we were told mail arrived and paperwork was there! Thank God I thought now I just prayed that we made it to him in time. Mickey had been gone for a long time this stretch but we didn't even stop at our home. We slowed down as we passed it for him to get a quick look then we headed straight for the hospital. We were approached by Mickey's brother and other family members, telling us that Grady was no longer responding, and that his blood pressure had dropped. We braced ourselves and headed in to the unit. When we reached his bedside he looked bad. Mickey spoke and for the first time in hours the nurses reported Grady responded! His blood pressure came back up for a little while during the visit. Mickey promised his dad that he'd look after Lee and me now. Mickey went on to tell him that he loved him and for the first time in Mickey's life his daddy said "I love you" back to him .I had to turn away and I choked back tears. In the past when Mickey would say I love you daddy he'd say "same back" if he said anything. Mickey asked his daddy if he'd made things right with God and Grady nodded. A preacher had been visiting with Grady at his home recently. We found out that Grady had prayed the sinner's prayer with him on one of those visits. Grady died that week. The death of his dad hit him hard. That would be the first of many things that would come against him immediately upon his release. Things lurked around the corner that we were not spiritually strong enough to handle. Anyone who has served God long enough knows that the devil sets traps for Christians especially when we are not equipped with our armor. I had pretty much tried to "set boundaries" with Mickey this time because I was tired of doing time and not having him home with me. He resented my boundaries and pretty much crossed ever line I had drawn. He drifted out of church and when that happened it didn't take long before old "friends" started coming around. He was working and driving a truck for his company to pick up supplies when a little girl drove her bike right under his truck. There were witnesses and all of them told him it wasn't his fault but that made no difference to him. He followed her to the hospital and called me from there to explain what had happened. Thank God the little girl was okay! Mickey wasn't okay though. He got her another bike. She even had our phone number so she could call Mickey and she did for a long time. He told me that he could still hear her underneath the truck and the awful sound of the bicycle being drug and destroyed. He was haunted by the incident for a while. Mickey had issues that most people didn't realize he had. He had problems going to cafes and sitting with his back to anyone. He didn't like the crowds of people at football or baseball games. Lee played both sports. He had little habits that he'd picked up from prison life but I learned to adapt. For example he insisted he needed a small trashcan beside "his area" in our home. So I placed one beside his recliner. It took him some time to realize the whole place was his area. He would drain shampoo bottles or lotion bottles by standing them upside down and making sure not a drop of anything was wasted. Pressures and stresses seemed to come at him from every side. These pressures were triggers. When people have lived a life of drug/alcohol abuse certain things (triggers) set them off. Only God can deliver people from these things. We'd been in "rough places" before but somehow this was different. One morning while getting ready for work I found drugs in our bedroom. I tried to talk to Mickey about it and he went into a rage. I was mad and I was hurt. I felt let down once again. He pulled up his sleeves and showed me bruises. He said, "if you want to see everything here it is". He had been shooting drugs at this point. I was about ready to call it quits but something just wouldn't let me let him go. I was hurt but I loved him still and everything in me wanted to save him. What I did was to tell him we'd get through Christmas and not mess it up for Lee then we'd see how things were. He lashed out at me as people often do to those closest to them when they are hurting. He told me that I had changed and was no longer the same girl he married. I wanted to control him everyone saw it too he said. His "friends and his family" had pointed it out to him he went on to say. Why couldn't he see I was trying to help him because I loved him? I carried pain myself. Couldn't he see that? Couldn't he remember that I had stuck with him through everything? Fear overshadowed everything I done when it came to Mickey. I loved this man with all of my heart. He was blaming me for all of our troubles. All I wanted was to have my family together and end this madness. I did time with him on the outside while he did it on the inside. Now it was as if none of that mattered to him as much as his friends. I realize now that the drugs had their claws sunken into him so deeply that he couldn't get free of them. He was ashamed of it that's why he'd tried to hide it from me. When I confronted him he didn't like it. Somehow we made it through Christmas and even had a good one together but in the back of my mind I kept thinking he would leave me soon. I had some routine tests done. He was getting more open with his drug use and had friends over in his shop when I got the phone call. A nurse called with my test results and told me rather matter of fact "we think you have a brain tumor your prolantin level is real high. I was being referred to a brain surgeon. I thought maybe Mickey was right and I have changed after all if I have a brain tumor couldn't that make me different? I wanted to run. That was my first instinct. I had to get to that lake and ride around it like I used to do. Thousands of things raced through my mind. He wouldn't have to leave me now but who'd help him take care of our son? I had to get out of here I couldn't catch my breath and by now I was crying. Through the tears I found my car keys. I couldn't leave him with all of those people and no one to watch Lee. I had to ask him to watch Lee. I knocked on the shop door he came out and saw me crying all I said was please watch Lee Mickey I need to go somewhere. He tried to get me to tell him what was wrong. I couldn't find the words but he kept insisting that I tell him. He was being real nice I thought but all I heard was the echo of his recent words about how I had changed. He wouldn't let me go just keep following me insisting I tell him why I was so upset. Finally I heard him say "please, Regina tell me what's wrong with you"? What's wrong with me? There it was it was me wasn't it? I heard screaming but I couldn't stop myself. I was yelling at him .You were right Mickey. It is me! I have changed! I have a brain tumor! I was hysterical by this time and shouting "and who is going to take care of my baby, Lee?" In my mind Mickey no longer needed me but Lee did. That was a lie that the devil had told me but I accepted it as truth. Mickey said "no way are you driving like this I am going with you, baby it's going to be okay I am with you" He pulled me close and held me tight. He said just let me get rid of the people and then me and Lee will ride with you around that lake. I hated that he knew me well enough to know where I was heading but then I was thankful not to be alone right now. He told Lee that I was sick but we were praying together and I was going to be ok. I realize now he had to tell Lee something because he'd never heard me yell at his daddy like that. He finally got me calmed down enough to drive me to the lake the three of us spent the whole afternoon driving first one place then another. Mickey refused to leave me through all of this. He stood firm even though he had been doing things that he knew wasn't Godly. He refused to hear an evil report from me or from my doctors. Even in his rebellion he spoke words of faith and covered me in them. He was true to his promise to see me through this. He went to every appointment with the doctors with me. He took me to the church and had people pray with us. Pastor Jack and my church family anointed me with oil and prayed the prayer of faith. Mickey made sure that my parents knew the battle I was fighting. I wanted to be prepared in case I had to have brain surgery. I had a cousin die during brain surgery. Once again I felt Mickey's love for me. He hadn't stopped loving me he was just fighting demons of his own. One day I came home from work and found him hunkered down in our room crying. He was a man of great physical strength. I didn't recall seeing him cry before except maybe when his dad passed away. He confessed that "he couldn't go on without me; it was me that held everything together for him". I had been trying to talk about what type of funeral I wanted and like things "just so he'd know". We had argued about it too because he'd refused to hear it. I had even told him that I'd help him pick out another woman to help him raise Lee if he wanted me to. I had been acting crazy myself just wanting to make sure that my family was taken care of. For the first time in a long time I saw he needed me and a fight rose up in me to live through this no matter what! My mom met us at the brain surgeons for the last appointment. He walked in there I sat with mom on one side and Mickey on the other. I took a deep breath and braced myself for his recommendations. I couldn't believe my ears. He told me the last MRI revealed that there was no tumor and I was fine. I had been healed by nothing less than a miracle! Even in our unfaithfulness God was faithful. In 1 Kings 18 Elijah called fire down from heaven then in the 19th chapter he was hiding in a cave from that evil Jezebel. It's as if sometimes we go from a place of victory to a dark place. That's what happened with me. I was happy to finally feel Mickey's love again. He'd told me before all of the health issues that he'd felt like he'd lost his friend. I longed to be his friend again. I knew that he loved me now and I wanted him to want me. I was lied to constantly by the devil. He was subtle and tricky. He told me that if only I were more fun Mickey would want to spend time with me. In desperation to be my husband's friend again I started dabbling in drugs myself. Mickey never told me this in fact he tried to convince me not to do anything. When I was high I felt as if I became another person. I didn't like myself most of the time and I couldn't understand why Mickey had chosen me. I tried to let my hair down a little with him. My self-esteem wasn't very good but had no insecurities surface when I was "under the influence". I thought that Mickey liked the person I became when I was like that even more than the girl he'd married so long ago. The drugs allowed me to hide as if they themselves provided me another mask. I couldn't look myself in the eyes. Looking into a mirror wasn't a problem as long as I avoided my eyes. See inside me somewhere I knew I was in this dark place and I couldn't free myself. I knew that I could no longer hear the voice of God in my life but I drowned those thoughts with more drugs. Historically drugs were associated with witchcraft. I believe that they still have demons attached to them. If we allow them into our households it affects the home whether we hid them or not. I won't elaborate on just how crazy Mickey and I got. Even the bible says that sin is fun "for a season". We did some things that we are both ashamed of but not a day goes by that I don't thank God for the blood of Jesus that covers all of that mess! Our season was about to change. Mickey was arrested the last time on a gun charge. The officer brought him by the house and returned my car to me. He allowed me to see him before taking him to jail. Mickey asked me to not let Lee see him like that since he'd never seen him cuffed. He told me "Regina I am sorry for all of the hell I have put you through I really am". I hugged him and told him it didn't stop my love for him. Once again I found myself doing time on the outside. He was taken to Geneva county jail to await transfer to prison. Then he was taken to Union Springs Alabama. In Union Springs all of the family members had to wait in line outside of a high chain linked fence. Around the top of the fence like most prisons there were rolls of razor wire. There were no gun towers visible here. It was in the line awaiting the visit that the decision to write my story was made. The line the families stood in was not only outside but it wasn't protected from the elements at all. It was not unusual to stand in the rain or the cold. Another inmate's family told me that they wished someone would tell the story about what it was like for the family members of people in prison. At this place we had to wait until the gate buzzed to let us in. That wasn't always done on time. It was up to the powers that be and what was going on inside before we were permitted inside. Then we had to go into small little rooms to have our shoes removed the shoes and the bottoms of our feet were examined. All females had to "shake their bras" when Lee had to go into the same room that I did he'd always giggle at that! Neither inmates nor visitors could wear jewelry of any type inside. I had to remove my wedding ring to visit this was really hard on Mickey. He was not accustomed to seeing my hand without my wedding ring. The fact that we were having marriage problems at this point only emphasized the absence of my ring. We faced heartbreaking days while he was here together. I was no longer sure that I wanted to be married to him because of some things I had found out. It didn't happen overnight but it was through much talking and praying that our marriage began to be rebuilt. It was as if we were both broken completely down before the restoration could begin. If not for the Grace of God we would no longer be married and I know that. Both Mickey and I rededicated our lives to God in 2005. He quit smoking as a sign for me that he'd give up everything for us. Our lives had come full circle and we were more like we were when we'd first gotten married. We have learned to be honest with each other even when it's difficult. Most of all we have learned to pray with and for one another. May God have the glory for what he is doing in and through our lives. It's not about us anymore it's about Jesus. Sometimes people hurt each other so much that they think there is nothing left but it was God that spoke the world into existence from nothing. He can do that for marriages if only people will allow him to. The process we went through was not one free of pain. We both hurt each other and we had a hard road to recovery. There is not a day that goes by that I don't thank God we stuck it out. On Thursday September 7th I made my way to the federal courthouse in Montgomery Alabama. I was thirty minutes early. I parked and filled the meter for two hours. I walked up the stairs and into the lobby. Two federal employees greeted me. I was asked to show identification and explain reason for being here. I showed my driver's license and explained that my husband had court today at 1:30. I was so nervous and sick to my stomach that I couldn't remember the judge's name. I told them my husband's name and they supplied me with the judge's name and what courtroom I would need to go to. (Courtroom 2-D) I was given a badge (#63) and directed around their desk and through a metal detector. The badge was to show that I had gained clearance into the federal courtroom. I got into a shiny gold elevator and pressed the button to the second floor. No one was in the courtroom yet. I was nervous I went to courtroom 2b just to make sure I had heard them right. No one was in that room either. I walked into the hallway and looked down into a glass case into the face of history. Memorabilia was encased and proudly displayed. Even the building itself was beautiful. I glanced down at my watch about ten minutes had made passed. I pushed my way through two sets of doors. The first set was made of glass. The second were heavy wood doors and they made me feel small. There was now a court reporter present. Mickey wasn't in the courtroom. I found myself a seat and eased down on the cold wooden bench. The chill of the seat seemed to go right through me. Others were making their way into the courtroom now. Mickey was escorted into the room but wasn't permitted to speak to me. There he stood right in front of me cuffed and shackled wearing an orange jumpsuit. He had heavy chains around his waist. His lawyer shook my hand. Finally the judge spoke and every one swiftly moved into action. Someone read, "The United States Of America verses Mickey Lee Moody". The reality of his sentencing had appeared before us. The process itself was almost overwhelming. This time I was alone in the courtroom. Our pastor had come the last time but it had been delayed. "Alone" was exactly how I felt. The courtroom was busy with words that went over my head. I heard this case number and that case number and so and so verses so and so...none of it made any sense to me. Law books were laid out in front of the judge at his request as he was trying to determine the "correct" amount of time that my husband was to receive for carrying a gun as a felon. After a little of arguing and lofty words they decided with what seemed like ease 180 months or 15 years. Mickey was allowed to speak then "to the mercy of the court" only he found no mercy awaiting his words. The sentencing was then pronounced again for fifteen years. It was followed by a lot of rules that he'll have after the fifteen years are completed. Mickey was now fifty-five years old and I couldn't help but wonder just how much a "threat to society" he could be in fifteen years. Lee our son is going to be twelve this year. My first thoughts were not about Mickey or myself, but how this was going to affect him. This day was long awaited for by the three of us. Mickey and Lee haven't been allowed to visit since November. He was held in Montgomery jail awaiting sentencing. It's odd but we actually welcomed prison to this jail because Lee would get to see his daddy once he was transferred to prison. At this jail, Mickey would be permitted to hand old letters to me through an officer. Within those letters he'd tucked gifts for us. We have received numerous cross necklaces fashioned from potato chip bags, strings from bed sheets, or jumpsuits. The inmates could dream up a lot of things to create for their loved ones. I have seen some beautiful handmade cards full of vivid colors. I used to wonder how they made things like that with those colors since no markers or things of color were permitted. I have since learned that they "pull" ink from other things by using hygiene products. I have often found myself shocked by some of the things I have learned that they can do. I have seen such talent in people doing time. Mickey was finally moved to what we thought was just a transfer center in Atlanta, Georgia. It turned out he'd have to stay there for years before moving on to lower level. I had to learn to drive in the crazy traffic there but I did it. We have had the advantage of seeing a lot of things because he has been in places like Atlanta. Fear may have stopped me from traveling there but since he was there I had to face those fears. The first few times I drove in Atlanta was terrifying! My knuckles were whiter than normal from gripping the steering wheel so hard. I always was glad to head back to our hometown. I welcomed the sight of freshly plowed fields. I didn't even mind getting behind a slow moving tractor after the craziness of the interstate. He went down in security level again. This time he was sent to Beaumont, Texas. We had to drive longer to visit but somehow we managed. While Mickey was in Texas I got another bad report. I had gone for a routine checkup. This time I was told that they were pretty sure I had ovarian cancer and were sending me to Birmingham to have a hysterectomy. The cancer center in UAB was supposed to be top of the line. I kept confessing that I would have the surgery there but they would find no cancer. My doctor in Dothan told me he'd pray for me. The one in UAB tried discussing where I would go for chemo after the surgery "if I needed it". I refused to talk about it with him. I stood on faith. There were times doubt tried to weasel itself into my thoughts. I recorded scriptures about healing with music and I listened to it over and over to drive away the doubt or fear. I knew that fear wasn't from God. I knew that he was still a miracle working God because I had already seen his hand in my life too much not to believe. Mickey was able to call my cell phone and check on me at the hospital. He had a hard time being so far away from me through this but he was thankful that my mother was with me. Together, as a family we have faced hardships. I believe it was because we stood together that our strength was multiplied. I read in my bible where we can put more devils in flight by combining our faith. We have learned to do the hard things to make the best of things for our family. If I could give anyone a word of wisdom it would be to never give up on your family because God has not given up on you. Do not let anyone tell you that anybody is hopeless. Because of what Jesus did for us we can all have hope.

www.ingramcontent.com/pod-product-compliance
Lightning Source LLC
Chambersburg PA
CBHW060853050426
42453CB00008B/968